THE CRY OF A SINGLE PARENT

*"Against The Odds: The Silent Strength
Of An Immigrant Mother"*

PATRICIA VERNA PAUL

ISBN 978-1-964165-51-6

Dedication

This book is a tribute to heroes who rise each day to face life's challenges with resilience and grace. It is a reminder that while the road may be tough, the impact they make in their children's lives is profound and everlasting.

Whether you are a single parent looking for encouragement, someone seeking to understand the sacrifices of single parenting, or simply in need of an inspiring read, *The Cry of a Single Parent* offers wisdom, hope, and the assurance that no one walks this journey alone.

A Tribute To Marie Virgin Paul

Marie Virgin Paul was a remarkable woman whose life was defined by resilience, hard work, and boundless love. A single mother, she poured her heart into building a life of purpose and strength for her family, embodying the true essence of determination.

Marie was a woman of unmatched class and poise, carrying herself with grace and dignity in every circumstance. Her intelligence shone through in her thoughtful decisions, her wisdom, and her ability to navigate life's challenges with elegance.

Known for her generosity, she gave selflessly to those around her, touching countless lives with her kindness and compassion. Her powerful presence was undeniable; she was a force of nature, exuding both strength and warmth.

Marie Virgin Paul was a steel-willed woman with a heart full of love, leaving an indelible mark on everyone fortunate enough to know her. Her legacy lives on through the lives she uplifted, the love she shared, and the values she instilled.

Forever loved, forever missed, and forever remembered.

Author's Note

Let this book be a voice for those who seldom get the recognition they deserve and a testament to the enduring power of love and perseverance. crifices. *The Cry of a Single Parent* delves into this profound and deeply emotional reality, shedding light on the struggles and triumphs faced by those who take on the role of both mother and father.

This powerful book is more than just a narrative; it's a lifeline for single parents who may feel isolated, overwhelmed, or unappreciated. Through heartfelt stories and insightful reflections, *The Cry of a Single Parent* captures the essence of what it means to parent alone,

Overcoming Financial Hardships: Navigating the complexities of providing for a family on a single income.

Contents

Chapter One:
Childhood Challenges

Sunshine. That's what my childhood was like. The mango trees were lit up by golden light, and the turquoise waves sparkled and warmed our days. By no means was everything easy, mind you. We got cuts from climbing too high, went off track on adventures, and had times when the path didn't seem so certain. But those were just freckles on a picture of a happy youth.

Even when I was a child, I was interested in many things. It made me discover secret coves and climb to the top of Pigeon Island's lush peaks. There was no need to prove anything, just a desire to explore what lay beyond the known. That could be why some things didn't go as planned. However, those unexpected turns and small slips made the journey even better. They taught me to be strong creative, and to enjoy the simple joy of new experiences.

This foundation, which was formed in the sun and through adventures, has stayed with me. This is why I was so open to starting over, and this is why I think that even the worst times can lead to something beautiful. What do you know? It's real. The problems I had to deal with later made my wins taste better and helped me see how strong I really was.

My story isn't really a fairy tale, but it shows how magical St. Lucia is and how strong a curious spirit can be. Don't forget that you are smarter, tougher, and stronger than you think. And sometimes, the best journeys begin right in your own backyard, with love in your heart.

My name is Patricia Verna Paul, and I hail from the beautiful island of St. Lucia. A Caribbean island is known for its stunning beaches and lush rainforests. As someone who has dealt with the difficulties of having dyslexia, I was glad to see that the island had a pretty good system in place to help people with disabilities. I was unhappy to learn, though, that this help did not cover people with dyslexia.

The disability support system on the island seemed to be more focused on helping people with physical disabilities. Those who needed them could find tools and make accommodations. But there was a clear lack of help for people with dyslexia, a learning disability that makes it hard to read and write.

It was fun to live with my brother. We were tight-knit and always ready to go on adventures. We climbed the Pigeon Island from time to time. We would go for a swim in the healing waters of the Sulphur Springs. The air was thick with the smell of sulfur, but the warmth of the water felt soothing on our muscles. Then, as the day came to an end, we found a great spot to watch the sky turn bright colors as the sun went down. Those times with him had been like magic.

Going to the beach with my mother as a child was a time I will never forget.

It was amazing to grow up on a small island, but everyone knew everything about everyone else, like the trade winds, gossip, and rumors that were sometimes true and sometimes not. As a child, it hurt to hear stories about other kids and myself, especially when they weren't true.

Thank goodness my mom taught me good values. The most important? Treat others the way you want to be treated. I thought that kindness would be returned at that time. It's too bad that wasn't always true. This truth hit me hard during my high school entrance tests, which are very important for all students in St. Lucia. As I concentrated on the test, the weight of the rumors remained, adding extra stress to an already stressful situation.

Concerns about my mother's health were always on my mind. I asked her about it because her behavior was strange. Even though her business was only a small diner and not a big restaurant, she worked nonstop and hustled in her own way. The most important thing was that the tiny diner made sure we had food, no matter how small it was.

People who came by our house would always ask my mom, "Virgin, could you please give me some food?" I'll pay you next week. But by the following week, they were nowhere to be found. They would avoid my mother because they had to pay for someone else, so they would avoid her. They wouldn't even come back and support her, would they? A huge amount of money was due to my mother. Oh, my poor mother. Bless her soul.

I loved running when I was a kid. I loved track and field. I loved the feel of the wind in my hair and the rush of adrenaline I got when I pushed myself to the edge. Things were different at home, though. My mom was strict and put a lot of value on schooling, manners, and good behavior. There was no time to slack off.

I had always been a tomboy. It never felt right for me to wear frilly clothes or play the quiet games that other girls liked. I wanted to feel the wind in my hair as I ran, the satisfying thud of a hit, and the sting of sweat in my eyes after going as hard as I could.

I got really into every sport I could find, from football to cricket. It felt great to prove people wrong and to know that I belonged on that field just as much as any boy. Wrestling? Sure, pin me down if you can. Boxing? Bring on the gloves.

Things changed little by little. It could have been the way I trained twice as hard as everyone else. Perhaps it was the pure happiness I felt when I played. The other kids chose to play with me because I was good, not because I was a girl.

Yes, I can handle everything. I'm good enough to compete with the best at both tough sports, like wrestling and boxing.

It was easy for my mom to say: "Be the best."

Of course, as I got older, I saw that I had a big problem: I couldn't read. This kept giving me trouble, and it became a regular battle.

Mom did everything she could to fix the issue. She put me in pricey individual lessons, paid extra for specialized reading programs, and worked with me one-on-one for hours on end, patiently trying to help me figure out how to pronounce words.

It just wouldn't click for some reason. I felt like I had failed all the time, which was very upsetting. It was hard for me to stay still in class when school turned into a war. There was a conflict between the need to move and let out all that pent-up energy and the expectation to be quiet and learn.

When I was a kid, I was a contradiction. The wind blew past my ears as I raced to win. I was a flash of focused energy on the track. I loved track and field and used it as a way to relax. But in a classroom, I was a lively soul who moved around a lot, my body buzzing with energy that I hadn't used up yet.

I drove my mother crazy as a young girl. I always fought with her because I was sure I was right. But there was a lot of pain going on underneath: the shame of not being able to read and the anger at being stuck in a world of words she couldn't understand.

Running became my way to relax. I could release all of my stress and anger on the track and use it for good. Every step was a relief and a short-term escape from my worries. It was freedom, a chance to be judged on my raw ability and drive instead of how well I could read.

It was always stressful for me at school, especially when I had to take tests to get into high school. I was stressed out, and everything seemed to fall apart around me. Teachers used red pens back then to mark mistakes, and mine always looked like it had red marks on it. Lots of zeros on my worksheets were a steady reminder of how hard things were for me.

GED classes from 9 AM to 2 PM? Absolutely not. The task seemed unattainable, as if they were conversing in a foreign tongue. I attempted the exam, and upon noticing the large red zeros, I realized I needed to take action. Thus, I took the same action that anyone would take in that circumstance - I discovered a method to enhance my score. I removed the zeros and altered the numbers.

When I was a kid, school wasn't as fun as it should have been. Yes, I did really well in math. I found logic and numbers very easy to understand. But everything else, especially English Language Arts (ELA), felt like a fight that would never end. It was hard for me to get good grades and keep my confidence up because I couldn't read quickly and easily.

Worst part? The being alone. In secret, no one knew about my struggle. I kept quiet out of shame because I didn't want to be called "stupid" or "dumb." I saw other kids breeze through their reading, pride lighting up their faces as they did so. At the same time, I was lost in a sea of confused symbols, comparing myself to others all the time and feeling like a failure.

I got really good at putting on a show to hide how hard things were for me. I'd act sure of myself to draw attention away from how hard it was for me to read. The constant performance was tiring, but the fear of being found out was greater.

I put on a brave face even though school was hard. I imagined being a young woman who was strong and wouldn't let anyone get to her. As a kid who liked hanging out with boys, I turned into a bit of a bully myself. It was hard for me to understand the social complexities of the world of girls.

Being an outsider wasn't something I chose to do. I just didn't get why some people, mostly girls, seemed to have a problem with me and why I couldn't fit in. I thought a lot, and I was always trying to figure out why things were so hard by studying my world.

In reflection, the answer was clear: I have trouble reading. It was hard for people with learning problems to get help on that small island in the 1970s and 1980s. There were no support services or classes for kids with special needs. If you had trouble, you were just left behind.

Every day in school, I felt like I was being set up to fail. When the teachers wrote on the board, it was your job to figure out what the words meant. I got chills every time I heard the words "tests," "quizzes," or "spelling bees." I knew what was going to happen next: more failure and more red marks on my paper. My grades were always bad, and school itself turned into a stressful and annoying place for me.

Seeing those red zeros on my papers all the time left a stain on my mind. Every test was impending doom. A sign that I would fail. The school wasn't fun; it was just a dull ache of frustration.

I became the class clown because of this. It helped me deal with things and take my mind off of how hard school was. Laughter became my shield and a way to protect myself. I made everyone laugh. I was the class clown. A lot of people were drawn to me, like bees to honey. You know, the person who is always making jokes? I was that person. Everyone in school knew my name! It was simple to make friends with that many people. Don't forget that I was also humble. That definitely built my popularity.

After that, there were sports. I was good at it. People were drawn to me like...well, even more bees to honey. I am not bragging, but I was really good and had a lot of friends.

Every new grade came with a big test, and then the report card was released at the end of the term. Mom, bless her, would be there to make sure I was learning. She would sit down with me and go over what I had learned that day. She had high standards and believed that I should always try to be the best at what I did. She embodied self-sufficiency. She was a powerful and formidable presence as I drifted through life without direction. She doesn't have a fancy college degree. Instead of taking an easy route, she chose to climb the ladder by managing supermarkets and other businesses. She was a true businesswoman, but do not be deceived by appearances. This was not a deal akin to a high-powered executive suite. From the very beginning, she was the type of person who understood the importance of a dollar.

So, I did what any child in a tough spot would do. When I saw those red zeros, I took out a pen and "improved" my number. A quick move that added another 0 to the failing grade, turning an F into a perfect 100. It was a bad lie, but it had to be told at the time. I couldn't deal with my mom's sadness, which showed in her eyes how hard things were for me. But I couldn't change all the numbers; that would be too stupid.

The fear of failing, the desperate need to please my mom, and the weak defense of being the class clown all became my reality. It was a secret shame that made me feel bad about myself and weighed me down.

I've always known that I was smart. Even though I wasn't very "book smart," I was quick, resourceful, and good at working things out. I often tried to trick my mom by using this to my advantage. I thought I was being smart when I played that silly game.

Mom obviously knew what was going on. She would get angry when she compared me to the other kids, like the kids of her friends who did really well in school and got into good secondary schools. At the same time, I was having a hard time keeping my head above water.

When I turned 14, the pressure really got worse. There was a very important test. If you did well on it, you would go to secondary school. If you fail it, you're out of the system for good at age 15. Back then, the only way in was to take expensive private classes, which my mom, being a single parent, couldn't afford.

She had tried everything: taking piano classes, tutoring, and getting help one-on-one when I was younger. But it didn't look like anything changed. My reading problems were always getting in the way, and anger started to show up around the house all the time.

On some days, Mom would be stressed when she got home from work, and my unfinished homework would cause a fight. The stress would rise because she was worried, and I couldn't explain my problems. This never-ending loop of anger and punishment wasn't a happy place to be.

"Get it together!" my mom kept telling me over and over. You're almost 15 years old, and you're still up to no good! Do you not think this is important?" It felt like a constant barrage of blame and accusations.

"Why can't I get it?" I'd ask myself as I stared at the words on the page that I couldn't understand. It was easy to do things like wash dishes and make meals. Reading, though? It was a wall I couldn't get over, and it looked like it could ruin my whole future.

Every time a future test was brought up, it made me feel scared. Tests had always been my enemy because they showed me how bad I was. When I was stuck in class, I would move around in my place and feel very anxious. The only place I could get away and feel in charge was on the track. Running was my safe place where I could get away from my worries and the fear of failing.

There was a small bit of hope in me even though school wasn't my strong suit. Just maybe, once I was outside those walls, things would be different. Mom, bless her heart, kept telling me how important it was to get my high school graduation. "You'll need it for everything," she'd add, "even to pick up garbage!"

I would try not to laugh in my head. What nonsense. Do you need a diploma to be a trash collector? In my naivety, I couldn't quite understand how a simple piece of paper could have so much power in the world outside of school.

Being blank. My mind was a wasteland, empty of the things I never knew. I did my best. I wrote words, put letters together, and did anything else to fill the room. At least I had nice handwriting. But what was written on the page was a mess of words that didn't mean anything and wouldn't answer any questions.

As I turned in my paper, I felt a cold confidence settle in. I was sure I had failed. I was sure of what I had done. I had failed more than just the test. The system, my own limits, and the future seemed to be slipping from my grasp.

I felt like a convicted prisoner when I walked into the exam room that day. A wave of hopelessness hit me as I looked around at the test papers and the rows of confident students.

Being blank. My mind was a wasteland, empty of the things I never knew. I did my best. I wrote words, put letters together, and did anything else to fill the room. At least I had nice handwriting. But what was written on the page was a mess of words that didn't mean anything and wouldn't answer any questions.

As I turned in my paper, I felt a cold confidence settle in. I was sure I had failed. I was sure of what I had done. I had failed more than just the test. The system, my own limits, and the future seemed to be slipping from my grasp.

When I was 15, the anger finally reached a peak. It didn't work at school, and the future looked bad. But my mom, God bless her, was always one step ahead. I could tell she had a plan because she knew the old way of doing things wasn't going to work for me. It was time to try something new.

Always, Mom had a strategy in mind. Despite the fact that I was feeling disoriented and defeated by school, she was aware of where I should be.

My life at school came to an abrupt end on a Friday, one week after I had completed my challenging common admission exams.

"You're not learning anything," Mom said in a sour voice. "It's time you found a job."

I was fifteen, had dropped out of school, and was getting a harsh reality check. I didn't really believe it at first. Was she really interested in this "job"? I was sure it was just a threat, a way to light a fire under me.

The last day of school was a Friday, which meant that summer break had begun. As June turned into July, the days seemed to stretch out in front of me like an empty painting. It made me think of lazy mornings, afternoons with friends, and the freedom that came with not having to worry about chores or school bells.

But when Monday morning came, my happy dreams were over. Mom, who is always practical, had other ideas. I went with her to a fabric shop, which seemed like an odd place for a teenager to be since I was wearing clothes that made me feel way too grown up.

As I walked in, I was amazed by how tall the bolts of fabric were and how full the shelves were with bright spools of thread. When I looked at them, everyone seemed very old. The women had knowing smiles on their faces, and their hands were worn down. I was the new kid in the store and about to start a new path that had a lot less doubt than I wanted to admit. This was my new school, and I was about to learn how to weave my future.

I could assist my family with my job. My weekly payment of fifty dollars was not given to me in its entirety. It was crystal evident that I was making a contribution to the household financially. At her discretion, Mom would refund a portion of it, but she would take the most of it. The amount of room for bargaining was relatively small.

Even though there were problems, there were good times in my life. For starters, Mom was great. In spite of her flaws, she worked hard to make sure we had a place to live and food to eat. She may not have had a lot of schooling herself, but she taught me to work hard and to believe that there was a better future out there, one that probably wasn't just on the small island of St. Lucia.

As the only girl, I always felt like a safety net for my mom. I was often the one responsible for everything. Being the girl child meant that I really took on the role of a mother and helped raise my brothers.

This meant I had to start my journey through "real life" early. The alarms were for jobs, not school. Before I really understood what was going on in the world outside our door, I learned how to cook, clean, and run the house. It made me strong and gave me a sense of freedom that would soon come in handy.

There was a sense of freedom that came along with having work despite the fact that there were financial constraints. While I was making money and making contributions, I was also beginning to carve out a place for myself in the world. This was a reimagining of what it means to be a teenager.

The job at the fabric shop wasn't really my dream job. My mind was full of dreams about writing-based jobs where creativity and sharing stories were valued highly. But it looked like every path had a big sign that said "reading required" at the start of it.

I had a big hole in my life because I couldn't read. In the days before YouTube and social media, reading and writing were the keys to information and chance. It seemed like a terrible joke—a world full of guides, apps, and stories just waiting to be read, but I couldn't get to them.

I didn't want to give up, though. I learned to adapt and use my secret tool, charm, to get around in this world. When I needed to fill out forms, I'd act like I forgot and show my best smile as I asked someone to "help a girl out." Most people felt safe around me because I was kind and humble, but there were always a few who admired my "differentness."

I knew I wasn't like everyone else, even when I was a child. It hurt to feel like I didn't belong, but I never knew where I fit in. How come I'm so good at so many things but can't do something as easy as reading? This question kept going through my mind and made me more determined to find my own way, even though it seemed like the world was trying to keep me out.

I had a different kind of strength, even though school was hard for me. I watched people and thought a lot about them. I could read people's body language and face expressions like a book. I was naturally good at finding the truth. This gut feeling helped me get around in the complicated neighborhood, which has its own set of unsaid rules and ranks.

I wasn't afraid to be unique. I wouldn't hesitate to stay away from someone who made me feel bad. I had a feeling that something was "off" about one of my neighbors. Back when I was younger, I walked right by her one day without saying hello. I thought it was rude, and it was a small way for me to protest against the strict rules of society.

And, of course, my mom found out, so she punished me. Because of what happened, I became more defiant. I didn't agree with the rules or the way things were done in the neighborhood. All of it felt unfair: the rumors, the critical looks, and the ease with which people hurt others' identities.

It wasn't helpful to be a girl. People started rumors about me because I liked hanging out with the boys more than the girls. It wasn't easy for me to grow up. It was always a battle: against my reading inability, against what people expected of me, and against the anger that came from not being understood.

I learned how to listen very well because I couldn't read. I liked being around older people and learned a lot from their stories and advice. They shared what they knew about the world, lessons from life, and useful skills with me.

It was always annoying that they couldn't get to books or libraries. Before the internet, people learned from reading books. But for me, books were strange things that were full of symbols I couldn't figure out.

I also couldn't write down my own ideas and dreams because of this. I could write—I could put letters together—but spelling was hard for me, and it seemed impossible to turn the sounds in my head into written words.

I had big dreams alone, longing for a future where my limits wouldn't stop me. A future where I could finally be free.

Now that I'm 30 and have kids, something weighs heavily on me. I still can't read. This wasn't supposed to happen. People thought that coming to America would be a step up, a chance to get better. But now I'm stuck because of something as simple as reading.

It makes me feel bad, you know? Because of this, I can't do some things I want to. I was so disappointed that I dropped out of the program. What do I have to show for having three kids? There's nothing. It looks like everyone else can do it, so why can't I? Not being able to read seemed unheard of. It looked like everyone around me had it together.

It's crazy because I had friends, a whole group of them, even in high society. They didn't know. Even though I wanted to fit in, I always felt like I was different and didn't quite belong.

I have had this feeling of being different for a while now. I have a lot of energy, and not everyone can handle it. It's times like these that really get me down. I get overwhelmed, and because of my struggles with reading, I can't even keep up. The words just blur together. I can write and express myself that way, but spelling always trips me up.

This has been a huge roadblock, especially because writing is such a passion for me. I know I'm a good writer, but the difficulty of reading holds me back. Over the years, it's taken a toll on me mentally, especially when it comes to the goals I set for myself. It's felt like a constant struggle, a personal failing.

I've had my share of hangers-on people who stuck around for whatever reason. I have no idea why. But it makes you think about the friends you have, doesn't it? The people you care about most don't always have your best interests at heart sometimes.

I vowed to myself that I would never leave the island and become as worn out from labor as my mother was. Still, here I am, following in her footsteps, despite my vow to myself. As a single parent of three little children, I must emulate my mother's tenacious work ethic to provide for my family.

Chapter Two:
Coping Mechanisms

We only had one teacher for everything in school back then. They taught everything from math to English to history to science. If you didn't get it, it was up to you to figure it out. There was no room for falling behind.

I was having trouble reading. But a voice always told me to stay ahead of the game. At least in my head, I could figure things out. That's why I kept my secret. I had set such high standards for myself, but I still couldn't read. I had to keep this a secret so no one would think less of me.

It became easy for me to make reasons. I'd say, "I forgot my glasses," as I sat at the dinner table. I knew how to act humble all the time. It worked for a very long time. In many cases, this plan helped me get by.

Interviews and job applications were the real tough parts. Reading became an important skill I couldn't avoid. It was true that I couldn't read, but that didn't worry me as much. It was easy for me to talk and explain myself. So the people I care about most, my friends, never thought anything was wrong. One friend didn't even know about it for 25 years! She didn't believe me when I finally told her.

"But you speak so well!" said my friends. My kids said the same thing. Most of all, my older son just couldn't understand it. "How can you not read, but you speak perfect English?" he asked me.

Now that I think about it, I guess I do act in a certain way. Maybe the way I talk has helped me stay out of trouble all these years. I really don't understand how I did it for so long. But hey, I did!

Now that I have three boys, I care a lot about their schooling. I was willing to put money into tutoring and the work. I was willing to do anything to give them quality education.

But technology wasn't as good back then as it is now. Do you remember the first Alexa? The one that cost a small fortune? Yes, I got one of those as soon as they came out. An answer to any question right at your fingertips? Genius!

While job talks were going on, those were my worst nightmares. I'd be a mess the night before. How am I going to make it through? I had an interview next month that I might go to, but all I could think about was canceling. Hours of paperwork? I could not handle that at all. And telling them I couldn't read? Not even close. It was just too embarrassing. I had carried this secret and weight around with me all my life. There is no way anyone would ever know if I kept it quiet.

As a child, I was very angry. Everyone in my class seemed to be moving on, getting ahead, and going to college. Me? Stuck. Even now, 50 years later, that anger still lives on. I still find this deep sadness hard to read, and it is mostly aimed at myself.

But here's the thing: I never stopped being angry. It never got in the way of what I had to do. I was always able to get around problems. Yes, there were times when I was mad that I had to call my kids for help while I was trying to read a book or fill out an application. Those times hurt.

That's why I'm here now. I'm sick of being stuck. I'm dedicating myself to learning so that I can finally break free from this restriction. Now is the time to move on.

I learned to hide things so well that you can't even imagine. Really, my whole life. Most of all at school. Nobody in my class knew, not one of them. Because I messed up my English class writing so badly, only my teacher did. I would either spell things by sound or put together odd words that made sense. That's probably why I'm not so bad at writing now.

Of course, the teacher knew. She would check my work and tell me which lines didn't make sense. But my teachers and friends didn't know what was going on. I knew how to hide myself very well. My kids even know what to do. "Oh honey, I forgot my glasses again!" I told them to get the menu first when we went out to eat. It took years of practice.

You would think that hiding that I have trouble reading all through school would have hurt my grades, confidence, and everything else, but it didn't. I kept my head up and did what I needed to. Of course, it kept me from getting a good education and following my dreams of becoming a lawyer or private detective. There was too much reading and relying on written knowledge on those paths.

But for everything else in life? It didn't hold me back. I kept moving forward, even if it meant getting creative to get by.

My reading problems kept me away from some social settings, especially when it came to public speaking. If I ever had to give a speech, I would find a way to get out of it. "Stage fright," I'd call it. I just can't handle the crowd." Or, say, "Public speaking makes me so nervous, I can barely speak at all, let alone read out loud." I told little white lies to save myself from embarrassment.

Church was the same. Reading from the Bible in front of everyone? Not interested. I'd be happy to help with anything else, like cleaning the hall or planning the bake sale, but reading from the pulpit? Never. They likely all thought I was just shy around cameras. I was "Verna, the shrinking violet." Nobody knew the real reason.

I also had many close friends over the years, but none of them knew the truth about my reading abilities. I was always able to outsmart everyone.

I once tried to ask for help by sharing my problem with a friend who was a teacher. I hoped she could help me find the right path. It didn't go anywhere, though. It was the same with this teacher I had for a while. I worked one-on-one with me, but I fell behind when life got busy. I recently tried to get back in touch with her, but she never replied.

I really don't know how to ask for help, and I have never been able to. I have always been strong and independent, able to figure things out on my own. It's possible that's a defense system that keeps me from getting hurt. I always say that the world is never nice, and others are quick to judge. It was just too dangerous to think that someone would find out my secret, make fun of me, or call me stupid.

That's why I built these walls around myself. I Keep everyone at a distance, especially when this challenge comes up. That way of life is lonely, but it seemed safer than the other choice.

It hurt my self-worth a lot to keep everything from people. It was like there was a big secret over my head, always reminding me of something I couldn't do. No doubt about it, it was embarrassing. Most of all, with the kids. I was still able to help them with their schoolwork. Luckily, their dad knew how hard things were for me. He would step in and handle those things. But even then, I had some doubts about how I'd done it all these years. Sure, I kept my head up, but still, there were times I felt like a fake. I really don't know how I did it now that I look back. It's just one of life's mysteries, I guess.

It's possible that I could have done better in school. I should have put more money into my education. But here's the thing: life throws curveballs. Putting food on the table and taking care of those three boys by myself was my first concern back then. It was just not going to work out for school. Being a single mom and going to school at the same time was like trying to keep your balance while handling many of life's difficulties. I wasn't sure I could handle everything.

That's why I did what I had to. I focused on the paycheck and kept moving forward. It wasn't perfect, but it kept our heads above water. There's no use crying over spilled milk. Today is a new day and a chance to start over with your story. That's how I see it. The future is where I'm setting my sights.

Every day, my boys see how strong I am. They see me deal with problems and show love even when things are hard. I may not have had the formal schooling I had hoped for, but I've learned how to be resourceful, strong, and determined.

There is no one way to get an education. The things that have happened to me in life have taught me a lot.

I never let anything stop me from progressing in life. I can read a lot of books, take classes online, or learn something new with my kids. Think about how inspiring I'll be to them by showing them that learning is something you do for the rest of your life. It is not just restricted to school. The experiences in life teach us to grow and keep moving forward.

I'm not going to think about the past anymore. I had to make decisions, and the boys I raised are great. It's time for me to look ahead. What would you like me to learn? What skills do you want to get better at? Now is my chance to write the next part of my story, full of growth, discovery, and the endless possibilities I hold inside me.

Chapter Three:
Dreams And Aspirations

When I was younger, I had a lot of dreams. I always dreamed of being a lawyer and fighting cases in court. I wanted to be a detective who solved mysteries.

The crazy part is that I still have that ability. I'm sure I could do those things. But the thought of writing on paper for a test makes me shudder. How should I go about that? How can someone with so many goals have trouble reading? I keep coming back to this question.

It could be because reading wasn't a big deal for me when I was a kid. I told myself over and over that I couldn't do it before I even tried.

You'll be surprised at how much more you observe when you can't read. Like, everyone else at a place looks at the menu, right? But I'm very interested in what people order and how they talk about it. It's fun to try to guess what the best meal is without reading the menu. However, dates are the worst. People are putting a lot of pressure on you to just know what you want. That's when I need to think outside the box. I'll sometimes listen in on nearby conversations in the hopes of getting a suggestion. Sometimes, I'll go with a gut feeling and ask the waiter what their best dish is. It's a risk, but I'm not just looking at the menu like I don't know what to do.

Years of living in that suffocating environment made me pray for a miracle, for someone to come along and save me. I went out with this guy. That was a mistake. He turned out to be a real jerk, and things turned out really badly.

Hey, that's always been me. Getting stuck in a bad spot? Jump. I learned that lesson well when I was a kid. I always had my goals set on something bigger because I was a hard worker. I didn't belong in that place or that life. You know, I had dreams. Huge, brave dreams.

It was clear what to do when things went badly with him. I ended things.

I was a thinker even when I was a child. I would think about things and get stronger, which I knew I would need. It was a simple truth: being weak on the inside could make you unable to do anything, whether you were blind, dumb, or otherwise.

It wasn't about having the most degrees or being the smartest. Everyone has dreams, gifts, and something they're really good at compared to other people. It doesn't mean someone is smarter or better just because they have a fancy title or a wall full of awards. A lot of people fall for it, but not me. Not the girl who couldn't read.

I went through a lot as a child. A lot of problems and difficulties. Even people I thought of as friends let me down and walked all over me. But no matter what, I stuck to a rule my mother taught me: treat others the way you want to be treated.

This strong desire to be good and prove myself turned into a habit. Yes, I did mess up a lot. But I stayed true to myself even when things went wrong.

Back then, I was in the city and looked at those bail bond signs. My one true dream is to hold a book and get lost in a story. That desire to read has been a steady pain in my gut and a source of constant frustration. Not being able to read felt like a curse.

In my head, I could hear my mother's voice saying mean things like "stupid" and "dumb." "Everyone else can do it, why can't you?" She would scream, and the spankings would keep coming in waves. I got in trouble for something I couldn't control.

As a child, I felt like no one got it. People on the street look like they have their lives together and are happy. But there are stories and fights that are kept secret behind that front. As a kid, I was stuck because I couldn't read. It was a secret load that I carried alone.

Most of the people around me had no idea what was going on. They didn't know about the problems I was having or the abuse I was going through while they tried desperately to "fix" me.

But that's when you need to step back and look at yourself. Self-reflection is very important. You need to look at yourself and your life.

That's right. The board needs to meet now. It was just me, myself, and I. You have to get used to being alone. You can't always depend on other people.

As a child, I longed for time to be by myself. I never got to go outside because my mom kept me on a tight leash. Stayed at home and did work all the time. As a second mom, I took care of my brother and even skipped school to babysit. It was all because I wasn't "smart." They thought that not being able to read was the worst kind of stupidity. I loved reading so much, but I was working like an adult while my youth was passing away.

But hey, all of those things made me tough.

It was hard to learn. Report cards? Forget it. They were too hard for me to read. The only things that made sense were math and track (I flew!). But reading? That thing was my weakness, and it made my mom and me mad all the time.

A Friday came around, and school was over. I had no idea that my mom had a "solution" ready. She was very friendly and knew a lot of people. After hearing about my "learning problems," she quickly said, "Can't learn? Get a job!"

The next thing I knew, it was Monday morning, and I was the youngest and newest worker at a downtown fabric shop. The fact that I couldn't read at all was hidden by the fact that my voice was the strongest. It lasted a year or two, but I didn't like jobs that didn't lead anywhere. You have to keep going and work hard. Plus, that job needed me to read, which put me back where I started.

"It takes a village to raise a child" was something my mom always said, but my village was very small—just my younger brother and me. When I was 14, I took care of a child before I even had my own. It was like having a second mom. A lot of people, both men and women, can tell this story. There are times when your parents set the rules, and there's no choice. They tell you to do something, and you do it. There are no questions or backtalk. My mom was like that; she was always on the go and taught us to be the same way. Are you a single parent? It's not all black and white. There are times when one partner takes care of the kids more than the other, even in married couples. The song is about not having anyone to lean on and feeling completely alone, even when someone is with you.

That was my life. It all began when I had to take care of my brother. Always busy and on the go. Plus, I had ADHD, which made things even more interesting. I was a ball of fire, boy! It was really, really hard.

I mean, I did have a job, right? It felt grown-up to work, like a step toward freedom.

My mom used to say that two male crabs don't live in the same hole. The same thing goes for grown-ups. You moved out when you felt like an adult. You had your own shoes, clothes, and money. And if they needed something done with those things, they didn't care about being nice. It said, "Hey, those are your clothes. Do X with them after you take them out!"

Same with the house. Slamming doors? Forget about it. You knew what awaited you on the other side of a slammed door. This generation, though? They get away with murder!

Growing up was a hard journey. Almost every night, I prayed for a hero in shining armor to come along and save me from my life. Eighteen could not come quick enough. Eighteen meant freedom and a fresh start.

However, reality always found a way to get in. What my mom told me used to make no sense to me. I thought I knew everything when I was a teenager. I kept saying, "She doesn't know what she's talking about."

It was crazy dating. There were parties, different guys, and everything else. The people I met were truly amazing and cared about me. Because I spent most of my life with other people, there were more people who loved me than who hated me. But sometimes, the people you care about most can turn out to be your worst enemies and betray you before you even know it. You think they're your only friends, your siblings, but they're not.

It wasn't new. It began when I was a child, and there were mean girls in my neighborhood. It followed me to school. It seemed like jealousy was always around me.

I always seemed to bother girls more than anyone else. It was hard for me to understand. Why didn't I fit in? I didn't fully understand until I was an adult.

We are all different. That's the truth. God made us all different, with our own skills and strengths. Just picture a world where everyone was a doctor or lawyer. It would be pretty dull, wouldn't it? Each of us brings something different to the table.

You need to figure out what you're good at. It does not matter what it is—tidying up, watching kids, anything! Not having a fancy degree or going to a lot of school doesn't help.

The important thing is to know what skills you have and use them because you need your own base, something that keeps you safe and lets you shine.

That thing, that evil spirit that kept coming back at night, was reading. As I lay in bed, letters would dance around in my head as I tried to figure out what the teacher had said. I felt like I could almost reach this knowledge. But by morning, it was gone, leaving me frustrated and empty.

This battle was with me all the time. Outside of my town, where people are very close, it is spread out all over the world. It's a fact that people love to talk about other people. The real question, though, is what they talk about. You will be called a lot of different names that don't even stick, and I can tell you that.

"Crazy" was a hit. They always called me crazy. Also, what does the word "crazy" mean? Since crazy people do crazy things, right? But I only talked and said what was on my mind. It wasn't on purpose that I was mean. I'm an open book. You get what you see. The same is true for what I say: I mean what I say.

And a lot of people couldn't handle that. It meant you were with the wrong people. There should be people in your life who accept you, don't judge you, and let you just be yourself. There were no whispers or side-eyes; there was just a real connection.

But that's what makes it hard: finding that kind of setting. It can begin anywhere, even with family. Because many of the things that bother you start in your own home. Family is where it all starts. Finally, there are people who are close to you and know your secrets and can use them against you. They are the only ones who can really crucify you.

Bear in mind Judas? The kiss? What was meant to be a loving act ended up being deadly. We need to be careful around people who show a lot of love, but something doesn't feel right. You should keep a close eye on them.

I've had a hard time with "tough love" my whole life. Threats and insults that are hidden as jokes and called names. "You're too sensitive," they laugh when you tell them off. People tell them, "Lighten up, can't you take a joke?" But making fun of someone is not the same as putting them down. An understanding? Yes, that does happen. But some things aren't okay.

When I was a child, I had to deal with demons and traumatic events that are now locked away in a dusty part of my brain. What do you know? I lied and said everything was okay for years. I put on a strong front and wore a mask. But there's damage that's been kept secret, a silent scream behind a carefully put-together front. No one can see it.

I started out young in life. Does chores, cooks, and does everything around the house. I learned how to be responsible early on. But school was where things really started to happen. By 14, things were getting tough. Fifteen meant only one thing: leave. Not a single if, then, or but.

"Get it together!" my mom yelled over and over. You're almost 15 years old, but act like a kid! Can't you pay attention in school? You never take anything seriously; you're always having fun!" The blame game never stopped.

And I kept asking myself questions. Why did I mess up? I should be able to do the jobs. But reading? It was made of bricks. Fifteen was coming up, and I had a big test coming up. I was so scared that I was bouncing off the walls in class. The only way out? The song. I felt alive when I was running. But the track wasn't the only thing I wanted.

I wanted law and private investigations. I was smart enough to do it—I was a natural watcher and analyst. I knew people couldn't hide behind fake smiles. I could read them like books because of the way they moved. Lies? There was a bad vibe coming from them that got under my skin.

It was there even when I was a child. Some people made me feel bad, so I tried to stay away from them. Like when you walked by a friend in the Caribbean. Respecting older people was taught to me; you always spoke to them properly. But this one neighbor? I didn't like something about her. I wasn't sure what was going on, but I knew I had to stay away.

Once, I didn't like this woman. She gave me creepy vibes. I didn't even say hello as I walked right past her. That was a mistake.

She ran to my mom and told her I had treated her badly. The next thing I knew, I was getting in trouble for not saying "Good morning." I couldn't stand that woman even when I was young. Even more so after she made my mom hit me over something as trivial as a hello.

It made me more determined to fight back against those useless rules and the people who had to follow them. The community's whole setup made me mad.

Don't get me wrong, we weren't going hungry. My mom did everything she could. She thought the best of me. I knew there was more for me than the palm trees of St. Lucia, though.

I learned by hearing because I couldn't read. Basically, it turned into a sponge that soaked up information from anyone willing to share it. Most especially the older people. Stories and lessons learned from past generations were important to them. That was a long time ago, before fancy libraries and social media. A good book was a prize.

The trouble was that I had too many thoughts and dreams to write down. I could write, but it was hard for me to spell. I couldn't figure out what the letters on the page meant as they moved around in front of my eyes. It made me mad, but I wasn't going to let that stop me. I really had trouble reading, but that didn't stop me.

The track was my escape. Every step was a chance to get away from my troubles. Because I had a lot when I was a kid, it was always hard to do well in school, especially in English class. That made sense, math. But anything that has to do with reading? Don't bother. It was a wall I couldn't get over, and it was always making me mad.

Sadness followed me to school. No one knew about the secret shame that was making me feel terrible inside. "Am I stupid?" I'd ask myself with tears in my eyes. Why couldn't I read like everyone else? The similarities hurt all the time. So I made a front, a strong and sometimes mean outside. I turned into a bully and a tomboy who liked being with boys. It was like trying to put together a puzzle that was missing pieces when I tried to fit in with girls. Why was I always the odd one out?

I had a lot of deep thoughts and was always looking for solutions in the world around me. And the most important question mark? My trouble reading. Things were different in the Caribbean in the 1970s and 1980s. There were no support services or special classes. You were on your own if you were having trouble. Pay attention in class and learn. Sink or swim.
For me, tests were the worst thing ever. I was scared of the Common Entrance tests, which were the way to get into middle school. To just hear the word "test" made my skin crawl. I was sure I would fail, which would mean another zero on my already long list of ones. It wasn't a place to learn; it was a torture cell. Every morning, I felt like I

could not breathe when I thought about walking through those doors. Teachers talk too much at the front of the class, making it hard to understand what they're saying. I didn't like school at all.

I wanted the American dream. A place where I could start over and rewrite my story. There must have been something in the water in the Caribbean that stopped me. The teachers might not have had the right tools. Back then, not being able to read or write meant you were really stupid. They don't use big words like ADHD or dyslexia. My only choice was to get away. However, I met a narcissist in America.

This guy was a skilled manipulator. All allure and insincere commitments. I spent six years imprisoned in a luxurious cage that he had constructed. He would cover me with love, a captivating mix of praise and admiration. I was the provider, the hard-working individual giving up rest for money. Working during the day was tough, earning $300 each time. Evenings were more challenging, a harsh twelve-hour shift in exchange for twice the salary. My existence was dedicated to constant work, followed by sleep and repeating the process in order to support his dependence.

I met my narcissistic partner through the kids. This winter was one of those sharp ones that get deep into your bones. My two boys were dropped off at daycare but not picked up. We did not have smartphones everywhere back then, but we do now. And because I was a single mom on a tight budget, I could only get myself one. At that time, the kids didn't have their own.

My phone rang while I was at work. It was a number that no one knew. Someone called me and said they had my kids. Right away, panic set in. But then someone told me that they forgot to be picked up from daycare.

At that time, I didn't think of him as a bad guy. He was just a nice guy from the street who offered to help. He said he could take the kids to daycare for me. He agreed, and his voice was so sweet and comforting. He seemed really nice and thoughtful. I felt calm and happy all at once. I thanked him over and over because my boys were safe.

As a parent, you know how scary it is for your kids to be alone and exposed. It felt like a surprise that someone stepped in to help in New York City, where anything could happen. He took care of my kids when I couldn't be there because he was there at the right time. It made me feel so good.

Following the event, I made it a point to meet the man and thank him in person. Then he told me something very scary. He told me he had been nearby for a while. He patiently waited for the right time to come into our lives. He got in right away.

Now, I'll talk about my ex-husband. I have three kids with him. We grew up in the same St. Lucia neighborhood and ran into each other from the time we were kids until we were teens.

He has a twin brother. As a child, I always told my mom that I liked one of the twins, but I never knew which one. They looked exactly the same, and even the women they were seeing couldn't tell them apart. It was really hard to follow.

Early on, I promised myself that I would not date a twin if I could not tell them apart. I had to be sure of who I was with. I took my time. My ex and I first became friends by getting to know each other well. We hung out, went to parties, and walked around town together. He was full of life and laughter, and he was generally so kind that it was impossible to avoid him. Do you know how it feels when you meet someone and just click with them? For me, that was my ex-husband.

I met him when I was 23. He was great to me. The surprise trip to France he planned for me was one of the best parts of our relationship. I had never seen anyone be so kind. That was something new someone did for me. That was so kind, and it made me feel really special. I didn't know how much he cared and was kind to me, and that meant the world to me at the time.

He was a very soft-spoken man. He never yelled or raised his voice and always kept his cool. That's how calm and collected he was. After being with him for six months, I got pregnant with our son, who is now 27 years old.

My mom wasn't happy about the fact that I was pregnant. She thought I could never find someone good enough for her. Every guy I dated gave her problems, and my ex-husband was no different. She never liked that we were dating. When he came over to pick me up, I remember it like it was yesterday. "This guy is going to treat you so badly," my mom told me straight out. I didn't know why she felt that way, but what she said hurt.

I told myself I would never have a baby under my mom's roof when I was 23 and found out I was pregnant. On Friday, I found out I was pregnant. That same day, I packed up everything and left. At the time, My ex-husband was living with his twin brother when I moved in with him. Even though there were some problems at first, we got used to our new life together. I was determined to give my child a safe home life.

Our house was close to my mom's boutique, which was on the street. I made it a point to visit her every day, even though I had moved out. Many things went wrong for me during my pregnancy, especially since it was my first child. There wasn't much I knew about kids or being pregnant. Back then, there was no internet or social media to use to find out things. I relied on my mom's advice and the opinions of older people in my life. I tried to spend time with the right people and learn as much as I could.

I took in information and events like a sponge. I believe I'm still that way. I can be alone in a room and observe everything going on around me, picking up things from other people.

My first child, a boy, was born on January 14, 1997. That day was hard to explain. It was full of happiness and peace. My ex-husband's mom was thrilled because it was her first baby, and so was my mom. We all loved our little boy very much, and he brought us so much happiness. He was a real gift, and we became a family during those times.

Our love was everything back then. We weren't fighting anymore because I had changed how I felt. It was clear to me how hard it was to carry a baby, give birth, and care for a child. I finally understood what my mom had been saying the whole time. I used to think I knew everything, but becoming a mom opened my eyes.

My ex-husband was making us a two-bedroom house while I was pregnant. We moved in together after the birth of our child. Back then, we didn't have much money for furniture, so we slept on a mattress on the floor. It wasn't fancy, but that wasn't important. It was enough that we loved each other. That's when my ex-husband asked me to marry him, and I said yes.

It was hard for me to make ends meet when I was 23. A very close friend gave me a wedding dress as a gift. Our rings weren't fancy, but our love was real and strong. That was the most important thing. Our wedding was a small breakfast affair that was both beautiful and easy.

Yes, the rumors began to spread again. Some people said in whispers, "Verna is getting married." They laughed and said it would end soon. People on the small island didn't have much else to do, so the stories spread quickly. Everyone was bored and always looking for something juicy to say.

I was happy when I found out I was pregnant, but it wasn't what I had planned. Getting an education was supposed to be my top goal. That is what I believe because my mother taught me that over and over again. I saw she was right more and more as I aged. Even though there were problems and delays, I understood why what she was trying to teach me was important.

I can see how much we grew and loved each other when I look back. What I had wasn't always perfect or what I had imagined for myself, but it was real. We built our life together on love in the beginning, even though we didn't have much else. That was everything to me.

I began to think about things more seriously as I got older and looked around more. I finally got it: my mom was right the whole time. It was I who was wrong. America was always a promise of something better and a light of hope for me. That wasn't my only goal—to be a mother, get married, have kids, stay home, and depend on a man. I'm not like that. I'm independent and don't need other people to help me.

People have let me down many times over the years. Family members and friends have all let me down in different ways. But my mom really looked out for me. I learned from her not to rely on other people. "Verna, you're a married woman now," she always told me...

even after I got married. You need to think like a married woman. You should hang out with married people instead of single people.

She stressed how important it is to be financially independent. She said, "It's fine to have a joint account with your spouse, but always have a plan B." "Always." Her words have stuck with me for a long time. You know, even though I'm fifty years old, I can still hear my mom's words. I'll always remember what she taught me and what she told me.

I didn't fully understand when I was younger. I should have paid more attention to what she said. I did hear her, but I didn't do what she said I should have. I didn't follow her rules and laws. But those words? They were right there in my mind. I heard them, and they changed me, even if I didn't always follow through. Her voice became a driving force in my life over time, reminding me of how hard she worked to make me strong and wise.

America was always the bigger picture for me. It is the land of chance. I had to get there. I thought about how I was going to do it all the time. I knew it wouldn't be easy because I think a lot. It's still hard to get a US visa. You can't just pick one off a tree. You need a ton of papers, like bank records, proof that you have ties to your home country, and everything else. Nothing is a sure thing, even if everything is in order. They can still say no. The application fees and trip costs add up to a big investment.

We had to go to Barbados to get a visa back then because St. Lucia didn't have a US embassy. One day, my brother-in-law told me he was going to Barbados to get a visa. He offered to bring our papers with him and try to get visas for all of us. I laughed at the thought. "Do you really believe you can just walk into Barbados and get visas for all of us?" Even though I wasn't sure, I gave them the papers anyway.

I was shocked when he came back with visas for everyone. It seemed like a miracle—a great moment of praise! But having the visa wasn't the whole story. What was really hard was finding out where to stay in America. I didn't have any close family in that area. Most of my American family was from my dad's side, and we weren't very close.

As I was in Castries, I talked to a woman about my plans to go to America but my lack of a place to stay. She said her sister was looking for someone to watch the kids. I grabbed the chance right away. It seemed like the best thing to do. I was thrilled. I could not wait to leave St. Lucia and begin a new life.

My husband was working on another Caribbean island at the time, and I had a midnight shift at a pub. It was hard for me to make ends meet, but I always had hopes for a better future. The American babysitting job was my ticket out, my chance to finally get to the land of possibility.

It was hard work working the graveyard shift at the pub, and since my husband was away, I had to raise our baby by myself. There wasn't much money, but my mom helped a lot. We were barely getting by from paycheck to paycheck. When I was in my early 20s, I looked at my life and said, "This isn't the life I want. This doesn't work for me."

I knew I needed to make a change because the place where I worked was dangerous. So when the chance to go to America came up, it was like a lifesaver and a pure joy moment. I told my husband about my plan when I got home and called him. I said, "I'll go up for five months and then come back home." That's what I did.

It was a lot harder than I thought the job would be in America. The duties were a lot bigger than they seemed, but I did what I had to do. I planned to stay for five months, but I knew I didn't want to go back to that job. What I had hoped for didn't happen.

I worked hard to make new friends before going back to St. Lucia because I knew I'd want to return to the US but not to the same situation. That's when I got in touch with my cousin. He saved my life by giving me a place to stay if I came back. There are people out there who really want to help, and that kindness stays with you. You remember both the good and the bad.

I only stayed in St. Lucia for two months after I got back there. After that, I went back to the United States and stayed with my cousin this time. The extra room didn't have a bed because they had just moved into an apartment, so I slept on the couch. For about a year, I slept on that couch and made it as comfortable as I could.

And I hadn't seen my family in a while. My husband was still out of state. In the end, I chose to stay in the United States. It wasn't possible to keep going back and forth, and I knew it would cause problems with immigration. Also, you can only be in and out of the country for a certain amount of time before your visa status changes. Setting up a new life for myself and my family in America, I was ready for the long run.

Being able to hop back and forth between the U.S. and St. Lucia was a red flag for immigration. After all the excitement, life in America was good, but the worst thing was that I wasn't with my family. I had no one to talk to and was feeling lonely. It's common to have that problem when you move to a new place by yourself. But I was still making money and sending some back to St. Lucia. I worked hard seven days a week. I worked seven days a week, night and day.

I finally asked my husband to stay with me. My cousin told me my husband couldn't stay with us when I asked him. He wouldn't let couples into his house. I was shocked.

"I'm married!" I thought. "How come you don't let couples in?" Even though it was annoying, it turned out to be a good thing.

I found a place to live. Even though it wasn't much, the fact that it was mine was a big step forward. Our two-year-old son came up with my husband. He liked it here, so he went home to get his things in order and then came back to stay.

I told my mom over and over to get her visa, but she tried twice and failed. She was really upset. Life often let my mom down, even though she was a strong person with big goals. A lot of people thought she was weak because she was kind. It made me think about how much our lives are like those of our parents. We tend to be the nice person, the single parent, or the person who works hard but never seems to get ahead.

I called it a poor curse that would last for generations. We worked hard our whole lives, but things didn't get better. I've always thought that I could break that curse. I didn't like having to follow rules and laws that weren't required. Why should I have the same problems my mom did? Her life was hers, and mine is mine. I was set on making a better path for myself.

When I think about the past, I can see how every problem and turndown led to new chances. I kept going even though it was hard. I learned to be independent, to take chances, and to make my own way. The past wouldn't define me, and the struggles of those who came before me wouldn't decide what would happen in the future. I was going to do things my own way and make things better for myself and my family.

Life was finally starting to come together. Things looked like they were going to work out. I had started school and was working. Things were going really well.

I was having a great time at a party one night when my phone rang. That call will always be with me. Your whole life can change with just one call. You can't move after getting a phone call; it can make your whole world fall apart. In fact, that's what happened when I answered.

I found out that my mom had died on the other end of the call. The shock hit me like a Mike Tyson punch to the gut. I got on my knees and screamed and cried. It seemed too good to be true. My mom told me the day before that she was going to surprise me by coming to America. She was going to be with me. She was no longer there. She passed away quickly, not even a day after telling me she would be here soon. There was nothing to warn them—no sickness, nothing. Just left.

The pain was too much to bear. I couldn't understand it. I couldn't help but think it was a nasty trick. It was too much for my mind to handle. She just said she was coming to see me, so how could this be true? My mind was jumbled as it tried to find a reason that made sense. A lot of "why" questions came up: Why her? Why now? Why me?

Back then, there wasn't as much study and treatment for lupus as there is now. My mom had a very bad case of it. It was hers, but she had no idea what was wrong with her. I couldn't fix the damage that phone call did to my life. It broke my heart completely.

I knew I had to go home after hearing the news. I went back to St. Lucia to take care of everything after leaving my ex-husband and son in the United States. I was the only girl in my family, so I had to do everything. I had to be the strong one and take care of her business. But I had to deal with more than just the sadness and the details. Plus, there was all the talk and stories going on around me.

People seemed always to have something to say about me. Today was no different. That has always been hard for me, and now it is again. There is a lot of talking and spreading of stories. What they said was just as important as the fact that they talked. Spreading lies is not the same as talking about other people behind their backs. Don't say anything if you don't know the truth. But people don't do that, do they?

It hurt, and there were whispers, but I didn't let that stop me. Before I could do anything else, I had to go home and take care of my mom's things. I felt like the whole world was on my shoulders, but I had to keep going. I had to push through the stress because it was here to stay.

It was the hardest thing I've ever had to do to grieve for my mother while also taking care of talk and other things at home. I wasn't going to let it break me, though. There was no way I was going to stop building my life and respect my mom, no matter how hard things got.

My older brother was there, and so was my youngest brother. The oldest, though, is always in charge and does what needs to be done. When I got back to St. Lucia, my family told me we should visit my mom at the morgue. They told me we had to leave.

I couldn't face it, though. I didn't want to go in. I was shocked when my mom left. It seemed like they were playing a mean joke on me to get me to come back. How could she be dead? It didn't seem real. At the house, she wasn't there, but I still thought it was all a trick.

When she died, I wanted her to look nice, so I bought her a pretty dress. I did everything I had to do even though I kept thinking it was a trick. I hoped that if I did it right, the trick would be found, and she'd be there living.

I will never forget the day of the funeral. I got ready when I woke up. It was harder to do it by myself. My husband, who is my best friend, was back in the U.S. We didn't have enough money for him to come back with me, so I had to deal with everything on my own, just like I had done many times before.

I put on all of my makeup that morning, even mascara, to try to look nice and put together. "Verna, why are you putting on mascara?" asked one of my cousins who saw me. When you cry, it will look bad on your face. I told her I wasn't going to cry as I looked at her. I had already cried enough. I was going to hold back tears at the funeral. There were no more tears.

I didn't even go to the funeral home ahead of time. I was unable to. I did not want to follow the standard steps. I was dying to go straight to the funeral and see who was really in that box. There was a part of me that kept thinking it was a trick. It was like my mind was playing tricks on me and telling me that everything was set up. Mommy couldn't be gone. How could she be? I didn't know why I had that thought. It's possible that I was too shocked to accept that she had died.

My heart was racing as I walked to the funeral. I was sure that soon someone would tell me the truth, that everything was a mistake, and I'd see her again. But I knew deep down. There was no way in my mind that I could believe she was gone. I had to check it out myself. I had to see her one last time.

A mammoth Catholic church in size. To the brim. I couldn't believe there were so many people there. Where was Mom able to meet all of these people? Everyone referred to her as "Miss Paul," and she used that name. This businesswoman, mother of mine, garners a lot of attention.

"Oh my God," I thought to myself, "what's going to happen next?" My only goal was to arrive at the chapel on time and look in the coffin.

After the car came to a stop, I made a break for it. Not waiting for someone to arrive. Yes, she was there within that coffin. Just then, it dawned on me. There is no going back. Really, Mom was gone. There was no trick involved here.

With a blow to the stomach. As if it were a low blow from Tyson, you know? I was suddenly taken aback by the news. Midway through the funeral, I experienced a blackout. Sobbing when I woke up, and then I passed out once more. The entirety of the event is a haze.

Who was present at that time? I was unable to inform you. It is only the crowd that I can recall. That is a heavy blow. Nothing could equal getting rid of Mom. For me, she was everything. My entire life.

There she was, lying in that stupid box, and there she was, too. Rage began to build up, infuriated with everyone. I was so enraged that I might have ruined the entire universe.

Such was the extent of the pain. She was not just my mother but also my closest friend. We were making preparations. Exciting experiences. There was so much to do.

Moving to America was the main focus of my dream. I want a better life and a new beginning. After I had finished settling down, I would have brought Mom over. To put it simply, that was the plan! In the United States of America, the country of opportunity, she would finally be able to find everything that she deserved.

We made plans for each and every day of the year. However, there are situations when those plans are not carried out as planned. In accordance with the proverb that states, "We make plans, God laughs."

This was not the way that it was supposed to be. My mind conjured up a vision of her here, with me, taking in this wild new world. Everything from my accent to the unusual food was a source of laughter for us. Now, however, life had different plans.

My mother assured me that she would come to see me. Watch as I construct this new life for myself. Then, in an instant, she vanished without a trace. The dream was gone. One moment, she was expressing her dissatisfaction with her chest, and the next, she had nothing to say. A straightforward cup of tea turned out to be a farewell that I had no idea was coming.

The funeral wasn't a good one. From one moment to the next, I would be arguing with the sky and demanding answers, and then I would suddenly pass out, only to regain consciousness at a different section of the church, bewildered and disoriented. The anguish was like a flood that washed over me and dragged me under. There was a thick depression that had sunk in, and it was so thick that I couldn't see through it.

Something was supposed to be different about everything. A new life in America, with my mother at my side. On the contrary, I was awash in sorrow, and the American dream seemed like a cruel joke to me.

It broke my heart to think about my little brother. When his mother passed away, he was just sixteen years old and there by himself. At the age of sixteen, I am confronted with the death of a parent. As a result of the fact that I had essentially reared him, I felt as though I had also lost my firstborn child.

My passion for that young man was unrelenting. On the other hand, love is not always a two-way street, particularly when it involves siblings. After pouring out your heart and offering genuine affection, you may find that the only thing you receive in return is agony. It reaches a point where you simply are unable to continue playing that game any longer.

Not just he was involved. Not even with my own children. You bring them up with the expectation that they will always be there for you, but in reality, life may be unpredictable. As they mature, get their own lives, and make errors, they grow up. It is not a problem; that is the way things are supposed to be.

On the other hand, it does make you want to guard your heart closely. You can't let people walk all over you for how long, can you? It is not a sign of weakness to be kind, and I am not a pushover. Never will be the case.

It was a turning point when Mom passed away. My own being was shaken by it. Presented me with an entirely fresh viewpoint. No longer would I have to answer to anyone, and I would no longer have to worry about being smacked on the head for speaking before my turn (even when I had a baby on my shoulder!).

Those days have come to an end. At the same time that Mom had left, any lingering sense of obligation had also left. All by myself at this point. As for me, I was prepared to face the entire world. There are no restrictions, and there is no holding back. I was the only one who could fight this war.

Many years passed in a haze of difficulties. Although I continued to make progress, life continued to throw me a curveball.

A moment ago, I was in St. Lucia, attempting to secure a visa for my younger brother so that he might travel to the United States. After that, the visa process was unsuccessful, and I found myself in a bind.

At home, there was a sixteen-year-old who was dependent on me, and I was responsible for him. We could not afford to abandon him. My hope is to return to the United States of America and find a job there. On hold for now. What started out as two weeks stretched into a month, and my employment in the United States was pleading with me to return.

What exactly was I going to do with this young adult? It was a blessing that one of his aunts offered to take him into her home. That woman is a genuine lifesaver. It was my promise to bring him over at a later time that I left him with her.

I did just that, by the way. He traveled to the United States and stayed with us for a period of time. He was a kind child who never got into any trouble and simply seemed to appreciate what he had. There are some people who never forget where they came from, but he never did.

Now, my ex-husband and I were in the United States of America. The loss of my mother, on the other hand, hit me like a ton of bricks.

I went into a downward spiral of depression, the kind that makes you forget to take a shower or brush your teeth. She passed away unexpectedly, which was something I was not prepared for.

I was unable to function because of my grief. Things did not feel well. I was filled with rage, not only at the world but also at myself. In my thoughts, I kept hearing the phrase, "Should have stayed home, and America wasn't the answer."

It was a battleground within my head. It was the kind of overthinking that leads you down a bad path, and it was swirling around like things like "shoulda, coulda, woulda." As a result of being unable to escape that depression, I became pregnant with my second kid.

On the other hand, it was a fun time. My ex-husband, who was a wonderful person, lavished me with weekly bouquets of flowers. Even though we did not yet have a house or an automobile, the little that we did have seemed to be just right; the best way to describe it would be as joyful and tranquil.

That is until another strike came. In the immediate aftermath of my pregnancy, I was given a diagnosis of lupus. As if it were a nightmare, I was rendered unable to move after giving birth. I was unable to walk, and I was unable to take care of the baby. My husband was at work, there was no one to assist me, and my newborn was wailing... it was just too much.

Things did not improve in any way. A week spent in the hospital, my husband managing work and daycare, and a new baby all at the same time... During that time, I was diagnosed with Lupus. I had preeclampsia as a result of the pregnancy, and I was also suffering from severe depression. I was a complete and utter wreck at the time.

But my ex-husband was there for me through it all. Then, all of a sudden, he also took ill. Since I was so unwell, I was unable to even take care of him. Every single thing seemed to be accumulating on top of one other.

It simply continued to come. My spouse became ill, and he became really ill. I took him to a number of different doctors, but none of them were able to diagnose the problem. This powerful and gorgeous man, who used to weigh more than 200 pounds, had begun to deteriorate.

Two years later, I found out that I was pregnant once more when I already had three children and lupus to contend with. Everyone is aware that lupus and pregnancy are not a good combination, and this particular instance was particularly difficult. During the entire process, they had me on steroids, claiming that it would not have any impact on the baby.

I was now dealing with three children, a sick husband, and a newborn baby. Sure, he made an effort to work in between bouts of illness, but with three children, the costs quickly piled up. Also, I was unable to continue to take care of him since I was carrying the weight of everything else on my shoulders.

The combination of high blood pressure, lupus, and depression was too much to bear. At night, when I was lying in bed and stared at the ceiling, I would wonder how much more I could possibly endure. No schooling, no documentation, and no social security; all I had was three children and a husband who was nearing the end of his life. Extremely upset about the world in general. That one person on whom I could have relied, my mother, was no longer there. It was just me waging this battle by myself.

Having to send my ex-husband back to St. Lucia was the most difficult thing. It was just too much for me to bear any longer. By the time he left, we had only twenty dollars left in our bank account. Here I was, with three children, a newborn, and no employment, in isolation.

Due to the fact that I had to go to work, the children started their day. Whatever it took, I had to do it for the sake of my family. I also want to inform you that God will bring some truly remarkable people into your life. After a long and difficult search, I was finally successful in securing a part-time position. This wasn't a permanent arrangement, but at that very moment, who cared? Not only did I require the money, but I required it earlier today. The only thing that mattered was making sure that food was made available.

It appeared as though things were finally beginning to be more manageable, but then life decided to strike me once more. For some reason, my employer, who is an incredible woman who has become like a second mother to me, found herself in a circumstance that disrupted my schedule. Seven AM to seven PM? With three kids?

For assistance with getting the children ready for bed and putting them to bed, I was able to get a babysitter. Those ridiculous hours were something I did for years, and I was a master at juggling everything. Everything was completed after work, including taking care of the children, going grocery shopping (since, hello, it's seven days a week!), and doing the laundry. To get things done, I would occasionally get up around four in the morning. For the purpose of getting everything ready, I would iron the uniforms the night before. When I think about it now, I have no idea how I managed to accomplish it, but I did, and I am proud of myself.

~~o

Chapter Four:
Transition To Work

I was a single mom in Bronzeville, Brooklyn. Having to build a life in the ghetto. We didn't try to hide the fact that this area was pretty bad. You quickly learned many things about life on those streets. But I grew up back in St. Lucia, and that's how I planned to raise my first child in the same way my mom raised me: strong and steady, even when it felt like the ground was shaky.

There were cuts and scrapes on both of our knees and hearts. Now, there was a whole new world with its own rules. These days, kids would say things that would get you into a lot of trouble back when I was their age. But what do you know? It taught me new approaches. I was patient with me and taught me how to be strong by hanging on even when the world seemed to be spinning too fast.

I was a girl filled with curiosity, but my reading skills hindered me. That was the heaviness resting on my chest, the sole factor causing me to question my own abilities. In addition to that, life was not too terrible. My mother had instructed me on the fundamentals so I could effortlessly prepare a delicious meal, maintain a clean house, and handle daily responsibilities. I possessed the necessary skills, knowledge, and self-assurance. However, when it came to reading and education, that's where I faced difficulties. That's when the uncertainties began to arise when the anxieties seized control.

As I matured, it felt as though I harbored a hidden truth, a sense of embarrassment that I couldn't rid myself of. I observed my friends effortlessly reading books, excelling in tests, and communicating fluently, while I found it challenging to understand the words on the page. Attempting to hold sand was difficult; the more I tried, the more it eluded my grasp. However, I remained determined and did not surrender. I worked hard, I kept going, and I overcame the frustration. Despite the difficulties, both past and present, I am aware that I am not defined solely by my reading skills. I am a woman who has a story to share, with a voice that deserves recognition.

Growing into adulthood has filled me with feelings of pride and achievement. I remember my childhood, waking up at 4:35 am to assist my mother in preparing for the day. I would help her set everything up, then get my younger brother ready, and finally prepare myself for work. During my childhood, I was constantly moving, never pausing to take a break.

Reflecting on it now, I can see that I became hooked on that high-speed way of living. It feels like a compulsion to me - when I'm not working, I feel the urge to be working. I've been coping with this mindset for such a long time that it's difficult to envision life in a different manner. However, it has both positive and negative consequences. On the one hand, it has motivated me to be efficient and reach my objectives. However, it is tiring and causes me to feel depleted.

In spite of the obstacles, I appreciate those initial encounters. They instilled in me the importance of working hard and being responsible, molding me into the individual I am now. I might be unfamiliar with myself beyond the busy and noisy environment, but I am eager to discover and understand my true self outside of my dedication to work.

During my teenage years, I felt invincible. I felt proud and empowered as if I were in charge of my own fate. Every week, I would proudly give away that $30, feeling like a boss, like I was on the right track. And I must say, it was a wonderful sensation. I felt proud of my ability to open my own bank account without relying on anyone else. I was the one leading the decision-making.

I was definitely not flawless. I committed errors and engaged in actions I shouldn't have taken. However, despite all of that, I felt proud of myself. I felt proud of my efforts, progress, and development. Mom was also pleased with me because I had mastered how to deal with her emotions and prevent any triggers. I was always looking forward and always striving for growth.

Feeling in charge and proud of myself was a fantastic sensation. Despite not always being correct and making errors, I was confident that I was heading in the right direction. I was gaining knowledge, developing, and transforming into the individual I aspired to be.

I got a job when I was fifteen years old, and I've been fighting my way through life ever since. I've been fighting the good fight since I was a child. You look put-together when you wear your wig, makeup, lipstick, and dress shoes. No one hears the cries for help hidden inside you. Everyone looks at you and makes assumptions about you based on what they see. The world is a scary place because you don't know who to trust or who will really help you. You can count on yourself more than anyone else at the end of the day.

I absorb information like a sponge, always eager to learn. Allow me a few hours, perhaps a few days, and I will become an expert. I will understand it, I will possess it, I will make it my own. I have a strong belief in myself that gives me confidence to know I can master anything. It's not only about acquiring knowledge but about excelling in it, mastering every detail. I don't like to waste time or procrastinate. I'm not slow; I pick up things quickly, and I absorb information fast. I will absorb it, digest it, and incorporate it into myself.

What's even better? I will be done quickly. I'll grasp it quickly, like a magnet pulling in metal. I will obtain it, I will possess it, and I will then proceed to the next task. That's simply my nature. That's just how I absorb information. Allow me an opportunity, give me an opportunity, and witness my success. I will acquire the skill, I will understand it, and I will accomplish it.

From my job experience, even with the menial tasks like washing, I discovered that excellence is the most important attribute. You must excel in whatever task you are performing. If I'm measuring fabric, I have to make sure to measure accurately with no margin for error. A small error, just one inch more, and I might lose my job. I approached my job with seriousness and took pride in my work. I consistently made an effort to stay on the correct course and execute tasks correctly.

The women in the fabric store felt like my own family. They were similar to my mother, my parental figures. They instructed me, they led me, and they pointed me in the right direction. I was an attentive student; I paid attention. I paid attention to their words, absorbing their knowledge eagerly. I not only heard but also actively listened and comprehended. That is what enabled me to excel in my career and succeed in life.

Being a single mom in a different country is like being in a whole new world. It was chaos in East New York, and I had two little ones hanging to my legs. There was not a single familiar face in sight. It was hard. Work and child care felt like a three-ring show, and the neighborhood was an adventure all by itself.

It was a nightmare to find safe childcare. That person looked you in the eye and said they would do anything to keep their word. Then, in the morning, poof! They were gone. Without a doubt, it was a test.

In the fall of 2012, people on the East Coast of the United States were bracing for impact. There was a huge storm coming towards the heavily populated shores of New York. A behemoth of a storm, born in the Caribbean and fueled by the warmth of the ocean, was barreling its way toward the densely populated shores of New York. Hurricane Sandy, a name that would become synonymous with destruction and chaos, was about to leave an indelible mark on the city that never sleeps.

The skies got darker, and the winds howled like a choir of banshees as the storm hit land on October 29. It poured down rain that looked like it would destroy everything in its way. New York City's streets were empty and strangely quiet. They used to be full of people and activity. The crash of wind and water was the only sound.

The storm surge, which was a wall of water that came up from the ocean, flooded the city's coast. There was a lot of damage left behind when the waves hit the shore and flooded homes and businesses. Lower Manhattan's streets, which used to be a hub of business, were now like a sea of water, with cars and other things floating around like toys in a pool.

The floodwaters shut down the New York City Subway system, which is a lifeline for millions of workers. Once a marvel of building, the tunnels were now a way for the floodwaters to get in. They came in like a flood, shutting down the system and leaving thousands of people stuck. The storm killed 48 people, with most of its destruction seen in Staten Island, including floodwater and strong winds. Another five people were killed in New York City due to Carbon Monoxide poisoning from using generators in their homes.

The storm came on a Sunday. As the weather reports changed, the city held its breath as the afternoon breeze turned dangerous. The word "subway closures," which isn't used very often in New York's fast-paced life, hung heavy in the air. Some people looked scared, but for me, it was just a cold knot of fear in my stomach. My daily routine was thrown off. There was more at stake than just getting to work on time. As a single mother navigating the city's underbelly, it was about the fragile security I'd built. The storm I was feeling inside didn't seem as bad when I saw that storm. But even that storm had to wait. Imagine, I walked to Lower Manhattan during Hurricane Sandy when the subway wasn't working.

It can be challenging to date, especially if you are a single mom. This one guy...well, let's just say he didn't like my exciting second son very much. My second son got my never-ending energy, which can be both a blessing and a curse. That's possible; your kids will sometimes end up having the same quirks and spark as you. And I can tell you, that spark in my son was very bright!

Thank goodness my job let me bring the kids with me. So, it turned into this crazy routine: the kids and I taking over Manhattan as a three-person team. I worked late at night and then slept for a short time before my alarm went off at 5 a.m. The Bronx will drop off the kids at school, take a quick run back to Manhattan, and do it all over again. At 3, it was time to go back to Brooklyn. After that, it was time to cross the bridge again. We did the same thing five days a week except for the weekends because the kids would not have to be in school.

When I think about it now, it was all hard work driven by love and a lot of coffee. You have to do what you have to do, though, right? In the middle of all that chaos and back and forth, there was a wild beauty.

Sometimes, when the city quiets down, and I steal a moment to myself, it hits me. Being a single mom in a new country and raising three little fireballs on my own has been hard, but I've made it through it all. "How did I do it?" I ask myself now. I really don't have a good answer. But here's the thing: I did it.

Little kids bless their hearts; they'll really test your patience. Mine were no different. But I learned early on, sometimes the hard way, that putting things off only leads to bigger issues. I became a "nip it in the bud" kind of mom. If a red flag appears, we deal with it right then. Don't wait for things to blow up or hope they grow out of it. My boys learned that you should always respect others and not cross lines. It wasn't always easy, but that clear line in the sand and early intervention helped build confidence and understanding. What do you know? My little crew and I became a better team as we went through life together.

Rules. They were my secret weapon. My three boys were raised by me, single and proud. I set clear rules and standards for them. Moving to a new country, having a hard job, and being a mother all at the same time wasn't easy. But I held the line, and by some miracle (okay, maybe a lot of love and a little guidance from God), they turned out to be really great young men.

There were times when I did question everything. But then I'd take a deep breath, look at the three little faces looking back at me with a mix of love and mischief in their eyes, and remind myself that I don't need other people to approve of me. I know what I bring to the table. I put together this life and family one brick at a time. And if I set my mind to something and did it, even if it seemed impossible, like raising good men by myself, then anything was possible.

Things wouldn't always be bright and happy. It would rain, and things would go wrong. However, even diamonds need a little push to shine brightly, right? In my heart, I had a fierce drive that made me know that we'd be okay. We've always been.

My job was my lifeline. It was the ground we were walking on and the roof over our heads. There were times when I did dream of things other than the daily grind. However, those ideas were very quiet compared to the loud roar of duty. My kids and their health were my priority.

Putting food on the table and a roof over our heads was the foundation. It wasn't enough, though. I tried to raise good people and teach them values that would help them no matter what problems they faced. It wasn't always simple. There were arguments and slammed doors, and there were times when I lost my temper. To protect my kids, I stood my ground like a fierce mama bear. You didn't have to be perfect; you just had to be there and show them what strength and resolve looked like.

I might not have had the time or money to try every option or follow every dream. We had limits, though, so I built a life around them. There would be love, happiness, and the peace of mind that comes from knowing I was living my best life, one day at a time.

Necessity became my first teacher. The world did not give me a long childhood or a peaceful time to follow my dreams before I had to start taking care of other people. Work wasn't just something that was talked about in school as a means of survival in the future; it was always there, buzzing in the background of my life. When I first started getting paid for work, it wasn't exciting, but it was real, and it taught me the worth of hard work and the quiet pride of being able to take care of myself, even if it meant giving up some of the carefree days I saw other kids having. When I was young, I learned a hard lesson that formed the basis of my character. It was the lesson I used to build my life and the values I taught my own children.

When Friday was over, signaled by the school bell, I barely felt joy. Fifteen. Or so I thought. I was almost an adult. Work wasn't just an idea anymore; it had to be done.

When I walked into the store on Monday morning, I got a little nervous. But that feeling went away just as quickly as it came. It was easy for me to feel at home in the store because of how friendly the staff was. It could have been my silly smile or the fact that I could make up a joke at any time. These women, who were mostly older than my mom, took me in and cared for me. I became the store's chief jokester, making people laugh or say something silly to calm them down. "Made a mistake, Verna?" they'd ask, and I'd come up with a joke that made no sense, which always made them laugh.

But now that I look back, I see I was just being cocky. I was fifteen years old and sure I knew everything. I was ready to take on the world, the shop, and everything else. Being too sure of myself was probably my biggest mistake at first. That's why those women were there, right?

To teach me, to show me the ropes, and maybe even to teach a young, vain person how to be humble and take responsibility.

Being fifteen made me feel like an adult in my mind. I was a "little miss know-it-all." It was my way or the highway. That was my arrogant state of mind, and let me tell you, it was a big, fat mistake.

Now you see why I thought I knew everything. I would even talk to this cute guy at work. Things were going great until he asked me to come over for lunch one day. Even better, a home-cooked lunch! It wasn't really fancy cake, but to a fifteen-year-old girl by herself, it might as well have been. Afterward, we talked. Every lunch break was an hour of not having to worry about my mom.

It was my dream to work in the city and make my own money, right? It wasn't, though. Not really. The fabric shop wasn't some magical launching pad for my future; I had to go there. Yes, my mom had rules, but trust me, they weren't meant to hold me back from being self-destructive. They were meant to keep me safe. I knew that deep down. Working at that shop wasn't really a goal; it was just a side hustle. I had dreams that went far beyond bolts of fabric and impatient buyers. But hey, you do what your mom says when she tells you to. You could not argue.

Mom got a job at the fabric store. It was not great, but $50 a week at 15 was a lot of money, so I decided to be grateful for this opportunity.

During lunch with the guy, I could be away from Mom for an hour without being watched. The lights in the city seemed brighter, and the streets were alive with a different kind of energy. I was free and able to do things here. I thought that.

We sat and talked after lunch until there was a nice quiet between us. After that, something changed. He put out his hand and lightly touched my neck, which made me cringe. It was so quick I barely had time to think. My first kiss. It was weird, cute, and a little scary all at the same time.

But that's where things got tough. He wanted more, and his touch lingered a little too long. It was easy to see what he was after. It hurt my heart to feel that. It wasn't supposed to happen this way. This rebellious, sweet afternoon was meant to be about freedom, not... Well, not what he had in mind.

You see, this "boyfriend" thing was new. I wanted to feel special and excited, but I wanted to do it my way. I could have been innocent, but that kiss felt like a line was crossed.

This guy forcefully and savagely grabbed my breasts, and his hands were all over me. I begged him to stop, but he wouldn't listen. I twisted my legs together like I was wringing a cloth, just keeping my legs closed so he wouldn't have access to my body. We fought on that bed as I struggled.

I fought till I got weak. I could not fight against the onslaught and decided to give up. That's how I got raped that fateful day.

The worst part about this was that I couldn't even go home and let mommy know I got raped. Because knowing the kind of woman mummy is, she was gonna whoop me. Because in the first place, she didn't send me to work to socialize with boys. Hence, I kept my mouth shut because I did not want to get in trouble. The terror gnawed at me, but I had nowhere to go. No one to confide in about the harrowing experience I went through. I carried such a big hidden wound at the tender age of fifteen.

After this boy raped me, he decided to torture me afterward. I was traumatized. I went back to the store as if nothing happened. Then I went back home as if I was completely fine.

My silence turned into a prison, a heavyweight that suffocated me. It was something I couldn't understand that he took from me that day. It made me feel miserable and dirty. In order to keep it a secret, I hid it deep inside my heart.

When Mom died, the scream inside me got louder. A quiet cry for help that could be heard in the space she left behind. But I couldn't find the words. That person was the only thing that kept me together. How could I tell her about the sexual assault that broke a part of me?

It became a habit to keep things inside. It could have been because I was by myself and I was by myself and only had two brothers to look up to. Maybe it was the worry about how she would react, that my pain would make her feel even worse.

I became an island of sadness, and the attack was a secret that I couldn't feel because I was so hurt from losing my mom. While the world kept turning, I kept going, stuck as a ghost in a life I barely knew.

It wasn't just the assault that was kept secret. They became a part of my life and a wall I put up around myself. Getting a bank account was one of my main goals at the fabric shop.

I never, ever thought that a fifteen-year-old like me would have one. But that dream got stronger with each dollar I saved. It was a sign of my freedom and a small fortress I built myself.

So, driven by desire and naivety, I walked into this fancy bank like a lost fifteen-year-old in a high-class jungle. Their minimum opening deposit was so high that I could never make it with the little money I had saved. I felt like a fool in a world full of rich people, holding my forty bucks.

The dream bank was out of reach, but the dream wouldn't go away. I was able to find a smaller bank that fit my needs. This story also became a secret. My mom never asked me where my money went, and I never told her.

It was then time for her to get her money back. At the same time, it was a test of the trust I was building up, little by little. But the fear of losing that account, that little bit of freedom, was greater. I lied and took her money, putting it in my secret safe place.

Even though the guilt was killing me, the silence remained. It was a sign of the future I was desperately trying to create, one in which secrets wouldn't be the only thing that accompanied me.

I had the account and was putting money away when it happened. I remember that she gave me money and then asked for it back. But I took the money and put it in the account. She didn't believe me when I said I put the money in the account. She believed I was not telling the truth. I'm in trouble again. I would get into trouble every day. I really tried to be a good girl this time, but I still got in trouble.

She didn't believe me when I told her the truth. We didn't have much technology back then, so I could only bring the bankbook. Mom didn't believe me until I showed her the book. It was what I did with the money she gave me. She felt awful. I could still see and feel how sad she was.

There were glimpses of light even when I was secretly having a hard time. Mom was so proud of me when she found out about my bank account. She had never had that as a young woman, and here I was, fifteen years old and in charge of my own little world.

The women in the store were like living, breathing life lessons. I took in everything they said like a sponge, even if it meant putting on my listening charm. Sometimes, I think I was a nosy kid back then. I loved hearing rumors just as much as the next person. But I had plenty to do at the store. There was no time to talk about everyone's lives since there were people to help and bolts of fabric to fold.

I guess that job made me grow up quickly in a strange way. I had to deal with responsibility, and I learned the hard truths of life a little faster than most people. One of the most important lessons? It came from Mom: always do your best.

That idea still drives me, even though I'm fifty years old now. My goal is not to reach an unreachable level of perfection but to give everything my all. Although life can be hard at times, and you may be dealing with secrets that could drown you, there is power in moving forward and being the best version of yourself that you can be.

That needs to be the best thing that has made its way into how I raise my kids as well. I taught my kids the same thing: give it your all in everything you do. But it wasn't just about them. See, that never-ending drive for excellence comes from my own youth.

I learned how to be responsible when I worked at the store. But there was another part to it that was driven by fear. Mom had a strong grip on reality. "Always be your best," she'd advise, "because even when you think you're grown, there's always a whooping waiting."

It wasn't a mean fear; it was more of a healthy respect for her limits. She didn't like to smooth things over, and her harsh voice kept me in line. I tried my best at work, school, and everything else. To be honest, getting Mom mad was something that was best avoided.

Always wanting to do the right thing and being on the right path became a part of me. When I became a parent, I gave it to my kids not as a responsibility but as a light. Giving it your all and always trying to be the best is an important lesson that can be learned from both love and respect for a good whooping.

It wasn't all bad at the fabric shop. It was like family with those women. They liked how easy I was to get along with and how happy I was. It was like a chameleon; I blended in everywhere I went. And now I'm here, I'm right at home. Everything was taught to me, like how to measure fabric, fold it nicely, and keep the trim station in order. I learned quickly and fit right in.

But here's the thing: the work wasn't a problem, but it also wasn't my dream. As the months turned into years, a quiet dissatisfaction set in. That wasn't the big stage I had in mind for myself. I was looking for something more, something that would make me feel passionate.

I really wanted bigger things. Bigger than cloth bolts and customers who can't wait. It was getting old to do the same things every day. If I'm not careful, I get bored very quickly, and the need for something new grows stronger every day.

I did it, then. I left. Give up. Well, let's just say Mom wasn't too happy about it. That's a different story, though. In any case, I left the fabric shop. It was the end of one story and the start of a new one that was uncertain but exciting.

At least not as often, Mom wasn't the whooping type of parent, after all. Maybe it was because I had a job and helped out around the house in ways she didn't expect from a fifteen-year-old. That fifty dollars a week seemed like a lot of money, but trust me, it didn't go very far.

She wanted thirty dollars for "expenses," which left me with twenty dollars for the whole week. That twenty dollars had to pay for food, the bus, and anything else a teen might need. As you might expect, "proper lunch" became a treat. What else could I do? It was her house and her rules. It wasn't possible to mess with Miss Paul, as everyone called her. She wasn't joking around.

My budgeting skills were great; I mostly brought bread and butter to work in brown bags. It wasn't perfect, but it was mine. That twenty bucks, my freedom, was a sign of the life I was slowly putting together, secret brick by hidden brick. Even though working in the fabric shop wasn't my dream job, it was a way for me to make a name for myself in the world. In spite of everything else, that felt pretty good.

My mom taught me to have strong morals. She always said, "Treat others the way you want to be treated." My mother was an exceptionally generous individual. Even though she had never been to college, she was very intelligent and clever. It didn't matter how difficult the situation was; she was the kind of person who would gladly help out anyone in need. Unfortunately, some people took advantage of her kindness in horrible ways. It's true that some people think being kind is a sign of weakness.

It's true that some people think being kind is a sign of weakness. Even worse, though? Some people were so insensitive as to attack her after all she did for them. It saddens me to think about it. The problem is that it's too easy for us to forget where we come from. Not me. The lessons my mom taught me are very vital to me. Even though I wasn't always grateful, her everlasting kindness has always been an integral component of who I am. I will always remember how strong you have to be to be truly giving, and I am thankful for my upbringing and the lessons I learned from such a generous woman. A woman who had so much light in her. A woman who shone like the sun, providing warmth and nurturing to everyone around her. She truly inspired me.

Before, I believed everyone was pulling for me. Every time someone came to rescue me, I attributed it to God since I prayed constantly for someone to come to my rescue. Whenever someone did come, I believed it was God's doing. But over time, I realized it wasn't God – it was the devil.

My mother's health was a constant source of concern for me. Her behavior was perplexing, so I questioned her. She worked relentlessly, hustling in her own manner, even though her establishment was just a tiny canteen and not a large restaurant. What was really important was that that tiny canteen ensured we had food on the table, no matter how flimsy it was.

Whenever somebody went by our house, they would always ask my mom, "Virgin, could you please give me some food?" Next week, I will pay you. However, by the following week, they had vanished. Due to their financial obligation to my mother, they would shun her in favor of supporting someone else. Not even to return and rally behind her, would they? People owed my mother an astounding amount of money. My poor mother. She deserves peace of mind.

I grew up in a small community named Moschydeh Margaret. My early years were spent in another area of the same name, Margaret Moschydeh Margaret. Raised by my incredible mother, Virgin Mary Pauldenne, I witnessed firsthand the strength and resilience of a single parent.

Being a single parent comes with its own unique set of challenges and triumphs. It requires resilience, dedication, and an unwavering commitment to providing the best for one's children. Single parents navigate daily life with both love and perseverance, balancing responsibilities and ensuring their children thrive.

However, single parents also have a powerful opportunity to give back to their communities. By sharing their experiences and insights, they can offer valuable support and mentorship to others facing similar challenges. Engaging in community initiatives, volunteering, and advocating for resources that assist single parents can create a positive impact and foster a supportive environment for all families. Giving back not only enriches the community but also strengthens the bonds that hold us together.

My mom was an incredible businesswoman who brought joy and laughter. She had the most genuine personality and the most hilarious sense of humor; she could make everyone laugh no matter how serious the situation. It was a tough existence, but she devoted herself to her job and our family. Tragically, she passed away, exhausted and dejected from working hard throughout her life, and it broke my heart.

I trust that God has a plan for my life. It's important to find what your passions are. Find something you really enjoy doing, no matter how dull it is, even if it is washing cars. God knows what each person needs and wants. My goals are different from yours. So, let's not feel envious when someone has gained success in their lives. No one can understand what another person is going through right now unless they put themselves in their shoes. You will never know the hard work they put in, what difficulties they faced, and how much they struggled to get to where they are. It's easier to drag others down but all the more

69

difficult to work on yourselves. Tearing someone down isn't going to make you more successful. Only toil and passion do that.

I don't like how people hurt each other's names by telling lies about their sexuality, sleeping habits, or cheating. Things like this need to stop. It leads to terrible things. When is this going to stop being so silly? Things are not going well.

It's weird that older people are more apt than younger people to do these things. Parents of kids of the Covid age have a lot of respect for those parents because kids today are different. Hats off to all of you!

It's been 25 years, and I still don't have the proper paperwork to stay in this nation. The fact that I am not a citizen of the United States has hampered every step of my journey. I work hard at my job all day and night to make sure my family has enough food. Raising my kids has been a hard journey that has required me to be selfless and determined all the time.

Work has always been a part of my life. In some jobs, I've had to use all of my strength and energy, and by the time I get home, I'm generally too tired to take a shower. I fall asleep while still dressed for work every time I sit down to eat. It takes place all the time. Since you've been giving your everything all the time, you're completely worn out. There are no words to describe how tired you feel.

Even though it's hard, I will keep going because I want the best for my kids. Every moment of stress and sacrifice I make shows how much I want to give my kids a better life. They are the light of my life, inspiring and giving me strength every day.

I've been having a hard time with Lupus ever since I was diagnosed 18 years ago, right after the birth of my second child. Lupus is a terrible illness. Please know how much your help and support mean to families who have had a loved one diagnosed with Lupus.

Despite my Lupus, I have to go to work every day. Because I have high standards. I do what it takes to take care of my family. I hate having to depend on other people when I can take care of my kids and myself. I have been let down many times, but I have stayed strong.

To all the other single mothers out there: don't give up. No matter how difficult the journey or how many bad days we may have, we must rebuke them in Jesus' name. Your family will be protected through prayer and the atoning blood of Jesus. Together, we can overcome our difficulties and endless responsibilities.

Those of you who have been victims of domestic abuse, whether you are a man or a woman, have my deepest sympathies. You must hold on to your faith because God is good, even when things are dreadful. Things that don't kill you make you stronger. We will also get through this.

There are no words to describe how sorry I feel for the families who have lost a child to gun violence. I can't even begin to understand how terrible your pain is.

And I really understand how hard it is for you as a parent whose child struggles with mental illnesses. We will also get through this. The battle is not at all easy. Please know that you can all overcome and persevere just as I did.

People talk about me, make assumptions about me, and wonder what's wrong with me. That's why I decided to write a book: to make things clear and calm everyone down. I'm going to tell you my story in simple words. There's so much to come in my story.

It's important to believe in God, pray, and worship. Have you ever been very sick all night and woke up surprised by what was going to happen? I thought of something while I was sick with a bad case of COVID. I thought, "Oh my God, I'm still alive," when I woke up. I was really scared that I wouldn't make it through the night.

Lupus comes with its own set of problems, but I've been through a lot of fights in general. I can say for sure, though, that God has never left me because I pray a lot. To be honest, there are times when I wonder how I made it through, and I have no idea. Mom, I'm so thankful for everything you've done for me. Also, all you illegal workers, please know that I feel your pain. Be brave.

I waited so long to get my immigration. I finally got my Social Security last year, and that's what I need to depend on now. At the same time, everyone else is working hard and getting by from salary to paycheck. That's how things are in New York—always working hard, every day. You'll see it if you've ever taken the train: everyone is running for Manhattan, Metro North, or New Jersey Transit.

We come to America in search of a better life because we believe it is a land of chance and wealth. But the truth is that it's just work. We're working hard, but we feel like the system has let us down. Take a look around you. It seems like the system fails us everywhere.

I recall the individual I once was - a defiant 13-year-old who had to put in effort to make $50. That event showed me the significance of effort and the value of learning. As I matured, I came to understand that all my mother's words were accurate. She had always stressed the significance of education, and it finally dawned on me why.

Through my experiences, I have learned to recognize the importance of putting in effort and staying committed. I discovered that in order to reach my goals, I needed to work hard and dedicate my time. It's not only about desire; it's also about being ready to work hard to achieve it. If I wanted to succeed, I needed to be prepared to give my all, and that's what I did. It's a powerful lesson that has stayed with me to this day. I'm grateful for those early experiences, even though they were challenging at the time. They helped shape me into the person I am today, and I'm determined to continue working towards my goals, no matter how difficult they may seem.

I have decided to return to school and begin again. I understand that it will be challenging, but I am still not willing to quit. I believe I still have a responsibility to carry out a goal to attain. I am not finished yet.

Admitting my weaknesses and working to overcome them requires a great deal of bravery. However, I am ready to do whatever is necessary to revise my narrative, revamp my life, and improve it. I am prepared to seize control of my future.

Chapter Five:
Social Dynamics

Growing up in St. Lucia, my mother was a force to be reckoned with. She was a party warrior, a woman who lived for the social scene, always surrounded by friends and the pulsating rhythms of the island. My grandmother would step in as the caretaker whenever my mother was out, watching over my brother, our cousins, and me. Being the only girl among four boys, I quickly developed a tomboy mentality. I didn't have a sister, and the idea of playing with dolls or indulging in girly activities didn't appeal to me. Instead, I ran with the boys, learning their rough-and-tumble ways, which made me resilient and tough in a world that didn't always offer gentleness.

Despite my surroundings, I was popular in my neighborhood. I had a few close girlfriends, but our interactions were carefully timed. We'd come together only when my mother wasn't around because the moment she stepped back into the house, the atmosphere shifted. My mother's presence brought with it a strict set of rules and regulations.

She was a disciplinarian, and there was no room for nonsense when she was home. So, my girlfriends and I learned to operate within the cracks of time, sneaking in moments of freedom when we could.

We had our fun, though. We'd gather at my place, help each other with chores, and then set about planning our little escapades. Cookouts were our favorite. We'd throw together whatever we could find, cooking up meals that filled the air with the scent of spices and grilled meats. But we always had one eye on the clock. My mother worked long hours, often returning home at five in the morning. We knew that we had to clear out before she walked through that door, so our fun was always tinged with the urgency of time running out. It was a daily routine, a dance of freedom and restraint, and somehow, it worked.

Looking back, I realize how much I enjoyed those days. My childhood was a mix of challenges and joy, the hardships tempered by moments of pure, unadulterated fun. Life wasn't easy, but it was good. I found ways to navigate the difficulties, whether it was through my tomboy antics with the boys or my carefully orchestrated hangouts with the girls.

As I got older, my social world expanded. I became involved in various community organizations—serenity organizations, as we called them. These groups were my escape, a way to engage with others and find a sense of purpose. There was no internet, no smartphones back then. Communication was a face-to-face affair, and if you wanted to see someone again, you had to plan it out. When I met someone, we'd have to set a time and place for our next meeting before we parted ways. There was no texting to confirm plans or calling to change the time. Once a plan was made, you stuck to it, and that was that.

I remember one guy I was seeing at the time. Our relationship was a series of carefully planned meetings, each one arranged in advance. We'd say our goodbyes and immediately start planning when and where we'd meet next. There was something thrilling about it: the anticipation of the next encounter and the need to be precise and intentional about how we spent our time together. It made every moment feel significant, every meeting a small victory over the constraints of our limited communication tools.

Living in Bronzeville, Brooklyn, as a single mother, I drew on the strength I had learned growing up. The neighborhood wasn't easy; it had its own set of challenges, its own rules that you had to learn quickly if you wanted to survive. But I was determined to raise my child the way my mother had raised me—strong and steady, even when the ground beneath us felt like it might give way at any moment.

There were plenty of cuts and scrapes along the way, both literal and figurative. Life in the ghetto was tough, and it left its mark on both of us. But it also taught me invaluable lessons about perseverance, about hanging on even when the world seemed to be spinning out of control. My child and I learned to navigate this new world together, adjusting to its rhythms and rules and finding our own ways to thrive.

In those early days, I often found myself questioning my abilities, particularly when it came to education. I was a curious girl, but my reading skills held me back. That was the weight that sat on my chest, the one thing that made me doubt myself. My mother had taught me the basics—how to cook a good meal, keep a clean house, and manage the day-to-day responsibilities of life. I had the skills, the knowledge, and the confidence to handle most things. But when it came to reading and learning, that's where I struggled. And that's where the doubts started to creep in, the fears that maybe I wasn't capable of giving my child the life I wanted to provide.

But I didn't let those fears hold me back. I was patient with myself, learning to be strong in the face of uncertainty. I had to be. There was no other choice. I was raising a child in a world that wasn't always kind, in a neighborhood that didn't always offer safety or security. But I knew that if I could teach my child the same resilience that my mother had taught me, we'd be okay.

As time went on, I found new ways to approach the challenges that life threw at us. The streets of Brooklyn were a far cry from the lush landscapes of St. Lucia, but the lessons I had learned back home still applied. I had to be strong, steady, and always ready to adapt. And so I was.

Growing up in the same neighborhood as my ex-husband, I always had a soft spot for him. He was the kind of guy who caught everyone's attention, not just because he was good-looking but also because he was a twin. That alone made him stand out, and the girls in the neighborhood were always buzzing around him. But from a young age, I knew what I wanted, and I wasn't one to sit back and let life pass me by. I had this go-getter mentality, a belief that if I wanted something, I could get it. It was just who I was—determined, driven, and never one to procrastinate.

I remember those days vividly, the lengths I would go to just to spend time with him. My mother was strict, and she kept a close watch on me, but I was always one step ahead. I'd tell her I was going over to my grandmother's house, which was true—to a point. I'd go over there, say hello, and spend a few minutes chatting, just enough to cover my tracks in case my mother checked in. But I didn't stay long. I'd pop in and out, just enough to give the appearance of a dutiful visit, while my mind was already on where I really wanted to be—hanging out with my crush, who would later become my husband.

Outsmarting my mother became a bit of a game for me. I was always ahead of the curve, finding ways to navigate around her rules without getting caught. If she asked, my grandmother could truthfully say I'd been there, even if my visit was just a quick stop. That gave me the freedom to spend time with him, often staying out until nine at night, which was pushing the limits of my curfew. My mother had no idea what was really going on, and I was determined to keep it that way.

But as careful as I was, there were some things I couldn't hide forever. I remember when I first became sexually active. It was a big step, one that I thought I could keep secret. But somehow, my mother sensed it. One day, she asked me to walk in front of her, just a simple walk, but she was watching me closely. I don't know how she knew, but the next thing I knew, she confronted me. "You think you're grown now?" she asked, her voice filled with that mix of disappointment and concern that only a mother can have. The very next day, she put me on birth control, making sure I understood that while she couldn't stop me from growing up, she could at least protect me from making any life-changing mistakes.

Being on birth control was a strange milestone. It was like an acknowledgment that I was no longer a little girl, even though I didn't feel quite ready to be an adult either. It gave me a certain freedom, but it also came with a new set of responsibilities. I was navigating this tricky path between childhood and adulthood, trying to figure out who I was and what I wanted, all while keeping up appearances for my mother and everyone else around me.

Despite the challenges, I found ways to enjoy my youth. I had a lot of girlfriends, and we had our own little world of inside jokes, shared secrets, and endless laughter. I was the jokester of the group, always ready with a quip or a funny story to lighten the mood. People liked being around me because I could make them laugh, and who doesn't want to be around someone who makes them feel good? It was a way of connecting, of finding joy in the midst of all the pressures and expectations we faced as young girls growing up in a neighborhood that wasn't always kind.

My friendships were a refuge, a place where I could be myself without the weight of the outside world bearing down on me. We'd hang out, talk about boys, dream about the future, and just enjoy the simple pleasure of each other's company. Those moments were precious, little islands of happiness in the sometimes turbulent sea of adolescence.

As much as I loved my friends, though, my heart was always with him. The crush I had on my future husband wasn't just a passing fancy; it was something deeper, something that kept drawing me back to him even when other girls were vying for his attention. He was popular, sure, but I never doubted that I could win him over. I wasn't the type to sit back and hope for things to happen. If I wanted something, I went after it, and I was determined to make him see me as more than just another girl from the neighborhood.

Life in our neighborhood wasn't easy, but it was full of moments that made me who I am. The laughter with my friends, the secret meetings with my crush, the way I learned to outsmart my mother while still respecting her—all of these things were part of the journey. They were the building blocks of my identity, the experiences that taught me how to be strong, how to persevere, and how to find joy even in the midst of challenges.

In the end, that crush I had on my ex-husband wasn't just a childhood infatuation. It was the beginning of something real, something that would shape the course of my life. And while not everything turned out the way I imagined, I wouldn't trade those experiences for anything.

One of the things that really defined me growing up was my sense of humor. I was the funny one, the one who could make people laugh even when things weren't going so well. It was a big part of who I was, and it drew people to me. The girls I hung out with loved my company, and we spent a lot of time together. We didn't go to parties all the time, but every now and then, when my mother allowed it, we'd hit the town and have a good time.

Things started to change when I began working. Suddenly, I was contributing to the household, bringing in money, and that shifted the dynamic between my mother and me. She saw me differently—not just as her daughter, but as someone who was responsible and capable of handling herself. This new sense of respect gave me more freedom, and she started letting me go out more often, though there were always rules to follow. I had a curfew, and I knew I had to be home by the time she set. But within those few hours of freedom, I made the most of it.

When I was out, I didn't waste a single minute. I'd go to parties, have a few drinks, and hang out with my boyfriend. I knew that these moments were rare, so I made sure to enjoy them to the fullest. Every time my mother gave me the green light to go out, I grabbed the opportunity and ran with it. I had a blast because I never knew when the next chance would come. That sense of urgency made those nights feel electric, filled with laughter and excitement.

Even though I had more freedom, I never lost sight of who I was within my group of friends. I was always the leader, the one who set the tone and decided what we were going to do. I think that leadership quality came from growing up surrounded by boys—my cousins, in particular. They toughened me up and gave me a bit of a manly edge, and that translated into how I carried myself around others. I was firm in my decisions and confident in my actions. When I said we were going to do something, my friends followed. They trusted me, and in return, I made sure we always had a good time.

Being in charge came naturally to me. It wasn't something I thought about too much; it was just who I was. Maybe it was because of the way I was raised, or maybe it was just something inside me, but I never felt comfortable sitting back and letting someone else take the lead. I had a vision for how things should go, and I wasn't afraid to step up and make it happen.

My friends seemed to appreciate that about me. They liked that I was decisive and that I knew how to take charge and make things fun. We had a lot of good times together, moments that I look back on with a smile. Those days were simple but full of life. We didn't need much to have a great time—just each other's company and a bit of freedom to let loose.

As I got older, those lessons stayed with me. The confidence I had as a young girl and the ability to lead and make decisions, these qualities became even more important as I navigated adulthood. Whether it was at work, in relationships, or just in the day-to-day challenges of life, I relied on that inner strength that had been with me since childhood.

In the end, I'm grateful for the way I was raised. My mother's strictness taught me discipline, but her eventual trust in me allowed me to explore who I was and what I was capable of. I learned to balance the two sides of my personality—the responsible, hardworking daughter who contributed to the household and the fun-loving, adventurous girl who knew how to enjoy life. Both parts are equally important, and together, they make me who I am.

Now, as I reflect on those days, I can see how much they've influenced the person I've become. The humor, the leadership, the determination—they're all still there, guiding me through life's ups and downs. And while I may not be that young girl anymore, the lessons I learned back then continue to serve me well, reminding me to stay true to myself and to always make the most of every opportunity that comes my way.

Chapter Six:
Misfortune

When I first got diagnosed with all those mental health issues, I couldn't help but laugh. It felt like a cruel joke. When the doctor told me I had bipolar disorder, I found it almost ridiculous. I questioned it over and over in my mind. How could I have all these mental health issues yet still be the mom who has it all together? My kids always called me the "perfect mom." That's how they see me because I'm always on point. I do what needs to be done for them, no matter what. So when I heard that I had these diagnoses, I couldn't reconcile them with the person I believed myself to be.

I remember thinking if I have all these mental health challenges and still manage to keep everything running smoothly, imagine how much more I could do if I didn't have them. The idea that I had these disorders just didn't fit with how I saw myself. It felt like it was something written on a piece of paper rather than a reality I had to face.

The only issue I've ever truly acknowledged is my difficulty with reading. That's something I've known about and struggled with my whole life. But the bipolar diagnosis? I never claimed it as my own. ADHD, though—that one I couldn't deny. I've had it since I was a child, and it's something that I've always recognized in myself. I know ADHD runs through me like a fire, shaping the way I think and act. But bipolar disorder? That one felt distant, almost like it belonged to someone else, not me.

My mother had a saying that stuck with me: "You don't claim it." She always said that just because a doctor tells you something doesn't mean you have to accept it as a part of you. Instead, you pray on it, you work to heal it, and you keep moving forward. That's what I've been doing all these years. I don't dress the way I feel; that was another lesson from my mother. She taught me that if you feel bad, you don't let it show. You don't let the outside world see what's going on inside your home or inside yourself.

For years, I've held onto that advice. No matter what I was going through, I never brought my problems into my workplace. I knew how to adjust how to keep things separate. I learned how to manage my emotions in private and how to let them out in a way that no one would know. I'd go into the bathroom, turn on the shower, and cry my heart out where no one could hear me. Or I'd scream into a pillow, muffling the sound so that it was just between me and the silence.

I've become an expert at putting on a show. My whole life has been about making sure everyone around me thinks everything is okay, even when it's not. I've gotten so good at it that sometimes I even convince myself. I can be smiling, cracking jokes, making everyone laugh, while inside, I'm barely holding on. It's like there are two versions of me—the one everyone sees and the one I keep hidden away.

This act has become second nature to me. I've done it for so long that I don't even have to think about it anymore. It's automatic, like breathing. But deep down, I know it's not healthy. I know that keeping everything bottled up inside can't go on forever. It's like carrying a heavy load that gets a little heavier every day, and no matter how strong you are, eventually, it's going to wear you down.

Still, I keep going. I keep smiling, keep pretending, because it's what I know how to do. But there are times when I wonder what it would be like to let go of the act, to just be honest about what I'm feeling. To stop hiding and start healing for real.

But that's easier said than done. It's terrifying to think about opening up and letting others see the real me—the one who's struggling, who's scared, who doesn't always have it all together. What if they don't understand? What if they see me differently? Those are the fears that keep me locked in this cycle, even though I know it's not good for me.

I've always prided myself on being strong, on being the rock for my kids and for everyone around me. But I'm starting to realize that strength isn't just about holding it all in. Sometimes, real strength is about letting it out, about being vulnerable, and asking for help when you need it. I'm still learning that, and I'm still trying to figure out how to balance being strong and being human.

So, as I move forward, I'm trying to be kinder to myself, to accept that it's okay not to be perfect, that it's okay to have flaws, to struggle. And maybe, just maybe, it's okay to let others see that, too. It's a process, one I'm still working through, but I'm getting there, one day at a time.

Growing up, I always had a sense that something wasn't quite right with me, even as a teenager in my late teens and early twenties. I could never quite put my finger on it, but deep down, I knew there was a problem. I used to sit back and analyze my life, trying to figure out what it was. I was good at so many things, but reading was always a struggle. It wasn't until much later that I began to understand what was really going on.

It wasn't until I had my second son that everything started to make sense. I saw so much of myself in him—he was practically a mirror image of me. When he was diagnosed with ADHD, it was like a light bulb went off in my head. That's when I realized that I had ADHD too. But back when I was a child, no one knew what ADHD was, least of all my mother. She just thought I was a difficult child, that I didn't listen. She didn't understand that there was something deeper going on.

After all the trauma I went through with my ex-boyfriend, I reached a point where everything became too much. I felt overwhelmed by the weight of it all, and I knew I needed help. So, I made the decision to check myself into a facility. It was there that I finally got some answers. I had always known that I had ADHD, but I never really understood the full extent of my learning disability. It turned out that I also had dyslexia, which explained why reading had always been such a struggle for me.

Even though I now had these diagnoses, there was one that I never truly accepted: bipolar disorder. The doctors told me I had it, but I just couldn't believe it. To me, everyone deals with mental health issues in some way or another—it's all about how you handle it. I often questioned the diagnosis. I've never been arrested and never acted out in a way that would lead someone to call the cops on me. So, I always felt like the bipolar diagnosis was wrong, a mistake on the doctor's part.

I refused to claim it as my own. In my mind, I don't have bipolar disorder. I've always believed that having a positive mentality is crucial, and by not accepting the diagnosis, I've been able to maintain my sense of self. I've never let it define me or dictate my actions. I've never done anything to hurt my kids or anyone else. I've always done what I needed to do for my family, kept my job together when I was working, and made sure everything was in order.

The only thing that has truly held me back in life is my difficulty with reading. That's the one obstacle that has consistently stood in my way. It's been the biggest challenge I've faced, preventing me from educating myself in the way I've always wanted to. But as for bipolar disorder and ADHD, they've never stopped me. If anything, the ADHD has been a blessing in disguise. I'm always on the move, always busy. I don't have time to sit around and feel sorry for myself because I'm constantly doing something. That drive, that inability to stay still, has helped me in so many ways. It's kept me focused on moving forward and making the most of my life.

But the reading—oh, the reading. That's the one thing that still haunts me. Even to this day, it's the biggest hurdle I have to overcome. It's held me back in ways that nothing else has. I think about how different my life might have been if I didn't struggle with reading. I could have gone further in my career, achieved more, and educated myself in ways I've always dreamed of. That's the one regret I carry with me.

Looking back, I can see how much I've been through and how much I've had to overcome. The trauma, the diagnoses, the challenges—they've all shaped me into the person I am today. And while I've learned to live with most of them, the one thing I haven't been able to shake is that feeling of being held back by my reading disability. It's like a shadow that follows me, always there, always reminding me of what I've struggled with.

But despite all of that, I've kept going. I've never let it stop me from living my life, from being there for my kids, from pushing forward. I've learned to adapt to find ways to cope with the challenges I face. And in many ways, I've come to accept that this is just part of who I am. I may not be able to read as well as others, but that doesn't define my worth or my abilities. I'm still capable, still strong, and still able to make a difference in the lives of those I love.

I've realized that it's not about the labels or the diagnoses. It's about how you choose to live your life in spite of them. It's about finding strength in the face of adversity, about refusing to let anything hold you back. And that's what I've done and will continue to do for as long as I'm able.

I want to share a brief story.

Mother's Day—a day meant to be filled with love, appreciation, and tender moments. That morning started just as it should. I was treated like a queen with breakfast in bed, the smell of freshly brewed coffee wafting through the air, and a tray adorned with rose petals. Everything was perfect. It was the kind of day that every mother dreams of. Lunch was a beautifully orchestrated affair, filled with warmth and the illusion of harmony. Dinner followed suit, a romantic gesture that made me believe, for a brief moment, that things were exactly as they seemed.

But the peace that wrapped around that day like a comforting blanket was soon to be ripped away. The night that followed would leave me shattered, both physically and emotionally. Monday morning was supposed to be an extension of the previous day's joy. We had plans to take the kids to a waterpark, a trip we were all looking forward to. The kids were excited, their little faces lighting up with anticipation. I was excited, too, but little did I know that this day would mark the beginning of the end.

It all began with a simple question, one that anyone in a relationship would feel comfortable asking: "Can you please help me with the kids' things?" The question was innocent enough. Packing up for a day at the waterpark was no small task. I was just asking for a little help, something that seemed reasonable, especially given how much we had to prepare.

But that question was like lighting a match in a room full of gasoline. His reaction was swift and fierce as if my simple request had triggered something deep within him. I didn't know it then, but that question was the spark that would ignite a night of violence and pain that I will never forget. His anger exploded out of nowhere. He started pushing me against the bed, back and forth, like I was nothing but a ragdoll in his hands. My legs bruised instantly, turning black and blue under the force of his blows. The man who had made me feel so cherished that morning had transformed into someone unrecognizable, someone terrifying.

I knew I had to get away. I tried to leave the room, my heart pounding in my chest, the adrenaline urging me to escape. I told him that I was going to call the cops, hoping that the threat alone would be enough to make him stop. But instead, it did the opposite. His rage only grew, and in a moment of blind fury, he swung his fist and struck me across the face.

The impact was like nothing I had ever felt before. I felt my face go numb, and then I felt it drop—the entire left side of my face seemed to sag as if it had been detached from my skull. The pain was excruciating, but the shock of what had just happened kept me from fully realizing the extent of my injuries. When I finally looked at myself in the mirror, I was met with a face I didn't recognize. My nose was bleeding, and my face was so swollen and disfigured that I couldn't even make out my own features. I looked like a completely different person, a stranger staring back at me from the mirror.

The next day, a friend came over. She took one look at me and gasped in horror. "Have you seen your face?" she asked, her voice trembling with concern. I hadn't, not really. I had avoided the mirror since that first glance, not wanting to confront the reality of what had been done to me. But she insisted that I go to the emergency room, and it was only then, sitting in that sterile hospital room, that I began to understand the full extent of the damage. My jawbone was broken, my eye socket fractured, my spirit crushed. The doctors told me that it would take weeks, maybe months, for the physical wounds to heal. But I knew that the emotional scars would last far longer.

We had been dating for three years, and during that entire time, he never had a job. I was the one providing everything—bringing in the food, the money, paying the bills, everything. Every so often, I would kick him out of my apartment, but we had this cycle of breaking up, making up, breaking up, and making up again.

Even after he broke my face, I still took him back. I remember when the cops came looking for him. He had been missing for days, and yet he was right there in my apartment.

Over the next couple of years, our abusive relationship continued. It was almost two years after he broke my face when the police came looking for him. I took that man and hid him under my bed. He was right under there, hiding. The cops came in and looked around the apartment but didn't find him.

He was so relieved that day. He had been considering jumping out of the window when the cops arrived, but I stopped him. I was on the second floor and told him, "No, don't jump out of the window. Come here. I'll hide you under the bed." And that's exactly what I did.

The cops even came into the room, looked me straight in the eye, and asked if I knew where he was. I looked right back at them and said, "I don't know where he is." And all the while, he was lying right under my bed.

Leaving that relationship was the hardest thing I've ever had to do, but staying would have been even harder. I couldn't let my children grow up in a house filled with violence and fear. They deserved better. I deserved better. So, I left, taking the first steps on a long and painful road to recovery. The trauma of that night still haunts me, but I've learned that healing is possible. It's not easy, and it doesn't happen overnight, but with time, support, and a lot of inner strength, it's possible.

In the end, I survived. I survived the broken bones, the shattered trust, and the deep, searing pain that came with being betrayed by someone I loved. But more importantly, I survived for my children and for myself. My story didn't end that night—it was just the beginning of a new chapter, one where I learned to stand on my own, to rebuild my life from the ground up, and to reclaim my strength and my dignity. And for that, I am proud.

Chapter Seven:
Reflections On Motherhood

When I look back on my life raising my boys as a single parent, I often laugh and wonder, 'How did I do it?' But in the midst of it all, I remind myself, 'I'm proud of you.' I would genuinely tell myself that because sometimes, you have to acknowledge your own efforts. No one else is going to do it for you. So, I always made sure to say, 'You're doing a good job. Keep it up.'

Raising kids on your own isn't an easy journey. I lost myself in the process, pushing my own needs aside. I stopped partying and stopped hanging out with certain friends. I cut people off, all because my focus was solely on my boys. And when I was around my kids, I was one person, but when I wasn't, I felt like I could let my guard down. That's the level of respect I had for them—I took motherhood very seriously.

Sometimes, I wonder if I was too hard on myself. Back then, if things didn't go as planned, I saw myself as a failure. And I hate failing. Failure is not something I take lightly; it's just not in my category. But that mentality weighed on me. Looking back, I realize, 'Maybe I should've been kinder to myself.'

One thing that always stuck with me was how my middle child reminded me of myself. Every time I had a parent-teacher conference, I'd find myself laughing inside. The trouble that child gave me was the same trouble I gave my own mother. I used to ask myself, 'Is this how I was? Is this the same trouble I caused?'

Raising kids is a two-way street. It's not something one person should do alone. Children need both their mother and their father. But raising them takes more than just two people—it takes a village. That's how challenging kids can be, especially nowadays.

I made sure to keep my boys on the right path. I'd always tell them, "The decisions you make in life, they'll follow you. So make good ones."

We had some tough rules in our house. No video games during the week. That was reserved for weekends only. And I never let them spend too much time on social media. It was too much of a distraction. "Focus on your future," I'd tell them. 'Life is going to be shaped by what you do today.'

Even now, at 51 years old, I can still hear my own mother's voice. 'Be the best you can be,' she'd say. And I'd like to think I passed that lesson down to my boys.

I always tell my boys, "You have to dream big. Never settle for less; always stay ahead of the game because life can be a game. Life will make you, and life will break you." And when life starts breaking you, you sit there wondering, "Where did I go wrong?" Especially when you're raising kids, it makes you question everything.

I remember the dreaded parent-teacher conferences. I hated going, especially for my second son. The moment I got that call, I knew I was in for bad news. "Notice something bad that boy is doing?" they'd say. I remember once the school called to tell me he was doing cartwheels in the hallway. That's how challenging he was.

Before heading to those conferences, I'd have three or four glasses of wine just to prepare myself mentally. I knew what was coming. But eventually, he grew out of it. Most of the time, they'll drive you crazy, but they do grow out of it. It's all part of the process.

Kids require a lot of patience. Raising them is no small task, and you need a reservoir of patience to get through it. I look back at myself before I had children—I was normal, happy, doing my thing. But the moment I had my first son, my whole life changed.

For 27 years, I put myself on the back burner. My focus was entirely on them. I remember when I used to dress up and make myself look pretty. I don't do that anymore. When I go to the store, I don't even think of buying something for myself. It's all about the kids. And looking back now, I realize that was wrong. It's totally wrong. You have to focus on yourself, too. Sometimes, you have to be selfish. You need to do it.

The journey of raising kids as a single parent isn't simple. It's not easy at all. That's why people say it takes a village to raise kids. And now, this generation is completely different. I honestly don't know if I could survive raising kids today. Kids now? I just don't know.

I used to wear dark sunglasses all the time. I had so many of them—different styles, different brands. And one day, one of the boys asked, "Mom, why do you always wear sunglasses?" I sat back and asked myself, 'Why do I always wear them?' It was like second nature by then. But I realized I was wearing them to cover my eyes. I'd be up all night putting things together—ironing school shirts, packing bags—because I always did it the night before. The night before everything.

That's just how it was.

I'd lay everything out the night before. That way, the next morning, I wouldn't have any problems—just get dressed and keep moving, especially in a place like New York, where you have to be ready to go at a moment's notice. It wasn't too difficult because when you're raising children, you have to plan your day. You have to think ahead. And it's not just with kids—it's life in general. You need to plan the night before so you're ready for tomorrow.

That mindset of always being ahead helped me raise my boys on my own. Raising kids can make you, but it can also break you. It takes a toll. Having children isn't something you just dive into; you need to plan for it because it's a lifelong journey. Kids need both a mother and a father. It's a two-way street.

There were nights when I'd be up crying, trying to figure out what to do and how I was going to make it work. And the next morning, I'd wake up with puffy eyes, still trying to figure it all out. That's why I always asked God for the strength to climb the mountains He gave me. Life felt like that sometimes—like climbing a mountain. It wasn't an easy journey.

But I acknowledge that I did a wonderful job raising my boys. I'm proud of myself. And I thank my mother because, despite being a difficult child, I still turned out okay. So, I tell myself, *It's okay for them to be difficult. They'll challenge you; they'll press your buttons. That's kids.*

Raising children requires patience—lots of it—and even more talking. That's what I did: a lot of planning and talking. The road to raising my three boys wasn't easy. I lost myself along the way and pushed myself to the back burner. I didn't matter anymore. The focus was on them, making sure they were on the right path.

Even at 51, I can still hear my mother's voice in my head, telling me to *be the best*. And I try to maintain that—be the best. But it's true what they say: kids can mess you up mentally, especially kids with special needs. They'll push you to your limits.

You have to plan for that journey. You have to be prepared because it's not easy. But in the end, it's worth it.

My journey of raising boys, especially in the heart of the ghetto in Bronzeville, was never easy. My youngest—strong, muscular—reminded me that they weren't babies anymore. One day, I tried to discipline him, and my arm hurt after I threw a punch. That's when it hit me—how quickly they grow up. In the blink of an eye, they're no longer little kids; they're young men. It made me realize you have to cherish every moment because once they become teenagers, they're on their own path, and it's either the right one or the wrong one.

You have to start from early on. From the moment they're toddlers, you work on discipline and guidance. That's what got me through. Sure, kids will be kids, but I'm proud that I made it. I'm proud of the mother I became.

I think back to my own childhood. My mother, being a single parent, always told us to eat before we left the house because she didn't have money. I never wanted to put my children in that position, to have to tell them, "I don't have money." I remember wanting a toy, an apple, or a snack and hearing those words. That stayed with me, and I made a decision early on to give my kids what I didn't have growing up.

That decision led me to America, searching for a better life. Being poor and raising children in this generation—it's a rough battle. I worked two jobs just so I could provide. Whatever my children wanted, if I could afford it, I made sure they had it. Violin lessons, tutoring—whatever they needed, I worked for it.

That's why I believe you have to plan when it comes to kids. Raising children is no easy task, and you don't just jump into it. It takes planning, commitment, and sacrifices.

Looking back now, through all the hustle and struggle, I can say I did a marvelous job as a single mother. And I'm so proud of myself.

⸜♾⸝

Chapter Eight:
Academic Struggles

Growing up, I couldn't read, and that reality weighed on me. It made me sad, angry and frustrated all at once. I remember thinking, 'Why can't I do something that seems so simple for everyone else?' I'd look at the other kids around me, the way they'd read out loud with pride, moving through sentences like it was nothing. It was like watching them walk on a path I couldn't even see, and that stirred a deep jealousy in me. I couldn't understand why it was so hard for me.

Every time I looked at a page, the letters felt like they were fighting, moving around, and blurring together. It was as if the alphabet was at war in my brain, and I couldn't make sense of it, no matter how hard I tried. And the more I struggled, the angrier I felt—angry at myself, at the words on the page, at the way nothing ever seemed to click.

At school, I just couldn't sit still. All I'd do was fidget, moving left to right, twisting around in my chair. When lunchtime finally came,

I'd run my heart out. It was like running could burn off the frustration, the restlessness. I'd run until I was so tired I couldn't feel anything else. Those runs helped, even just a little, letting the tension in my chest loosen and fade. But then I'd be back in class, staring at the pages again, and the letters would start their dance, each one mocking me.

Math, though, was different. Numbers didn't move around like the letters did. They stayed in their place, lined up neatly, solid, and predictable. I could handle numbers; I was good at math. There was a sense of calm in solving problems with numbers, something that I couldn't find with words.

One day, my teacher noticed my restlessness. "Why are you always moving around?" she asked.

I shrugged, avoiding her eyes. 'How could I explain that the alphabet was a battlefield?' When I looked at the words, they seemed to scatter like pieces in a puzzle I couldn't solve.

Those early years were full of that same battle. Reading felt like a wall I couldn't get over, a constant reminder of what I couldn't do. But there was one thing I could do: I could run. Running let me feel a little freer, a little more in control. And I clung to that. So yeah, math was something I had no problem doing.

But reading—that just wouldn't come to me. No matter how hard I tried, I couldn't get it. 'What's wrong with me? Why can't I read?' That question followed me everywhere, especially in school. It felt like everyone else could read so easily, moving through stories and lessons while I stayed stuck. And every time I'd struggle, I'd hear my mother's words echo in my mind.

"Why can't you be more like the other kids?" she'd ask, her voice sharp with disappointment. "They're all doing so well. What's wrong with you?" Sometimes, she'd even call me "stupid." And, honestly, I believed it. I started to think maybe she was right—maybe there was something wrong with me.

Seeing the other kids read, seeing them do well, filled me with jealousy I couldn't control. They'd pass exams and move on to secondary school while I stayed behind. It was like I was stuck on one side of a river, watching everyone else cross to the other. Reading was this bridge I couldn't seem to build, no matter how many times I tried.

The anger that built up in me was so strong. Every day at school, I was tense and ready to snap, especially with the kids who did better than me. I remember one girl in particular—one of the smartest in the class. She'd sit there quietly, her head bent over her book, reading out loud like it was the easiest thing in the world. And I couldn't stand it. One day, as she sat on the bench, I walked over and, without a second thought, pulled her hair. I was so full of anger and jealousy that it just spilled over.

She'd turn around, wide-eyed, and ask, "What's wrong with you?" But what could I say? How could I explain this frustration, this deep feeling of not measuring up?

And the question never left me: 'Why can't I read? What's happening in my brain that makes the letters dance and jump around?' To this day, it's been a constant struggle, something that's followed me into adulthood.

At night, lying in bed, I'd replay the day at school over and over, trying to go over what the teacher had taught. It was like I was a sponge, soaking up every detail, trying to memorize everything that happened in the classroom. But by morning, it was all gone, just blank. I couldn't remember a thing like the lessons had slipped right out of my mind as I slept. I'd sit in class, staring at my open book, and all I could see was the alphabet doing some sort of dance in my brain. The letters would just twist and turn, moving in ways that I couldn't make sense of.

I couldn't stay still, either, not in my seat and not even for a moment. I was constantly shifting around, fidgeting, anything to try to burn off some of that restless energy. My mind felt like a river, always moving and never settling. I'd look around at the other kids, sitting calmly, and wonder, 'Why can't I just sit still and focus like they do?'

Running was the one thing that helped. Out on the track, I could finally let go of everything that made me feel so different and lost in the classroom. Running calmed me down in a way nothing else could. The movement, the wind, the rhythm of my feet hitting the ground— it brought me a sense of peace and clarity. When I ran, my mind didn't feel like a battlefield. It felt free.

Back then, no one in the Caribbean knew about ADHD or learning disorders. There wasn't any understanding of "hyperactivity." To everyone around me, it was simple: you either could read or you couldn't. And if you couldn't, well, that meant you were just *dumb* or *lazy.* That's all anyone saw.

People didn't realize how hard I was trying. They didn't see the way I would try and memorize every word on the page, going over and over it, hoping something would stick. All they saw was the result: a kid who couldn't read, couldn't sit still, and didn't seem to understand what everyone else picked up so easily.

The struggle to learn was real, and it held me back in so many ways. Education became this big, steep hill I could never quite climb. It felt like no matter how hard I tried, I would always slip back down to the bottom.

Growing up with my reading challenges, there was never a solution. No one had answers for my hyperactivity, either. It felt like all I got was the constant reminder of what I couldn't do. Math was fine—I could handle numbers—but when it came to spelling, reading, or writing, it was like my mind hit a wall. I'd sit there, trying my hardest, and when I couldn't get it, I would cry. I cried so many times, tears of frustration and anger because of my reading struggles. I'd wonder, over and over, 'Why can't I get this?'

There were times I had extra lessons, and I'd go in with some hope, thinking maybe this time, maybe 'this' would be the help I needed. But nothing worked. After so many attempts, I finally reached a breaking point. I remember thinking, 'Enough is enough. Just leave it alone.' It was exhausting, and the embarrassment only made it worse. Reading aloud, like giving a speech or reading the Bible, felt like I was exposing my biggest secret to everyone.

So, I kept it hidden. I didn't let anyone know about my struggle with reading; I held it in and kept it to myself. And here I am, still without a real solution. Even now, I wonder what it is about my brain that makes reading feel like such a battle.

And the hyperactivity—it's still there, even at 51. When I'm not active or keeping busy, a sadness creeps in. I can't sit still or do anything; it's like I'm addicted to staying active. If I slow down, the quietness weighs heavy, and I start feeling down, even depressed. It's as if the only way to feel okay is to keep moving, keep busy, and always do something. It's a habit I haven't been able to break, a kind of restlessness that's part of me.